Easy Name Change

The guide to changing your name after marriage

Congratulations on your special day!

The New Name name change kit makes your name change easy. We've done the research and investigated the name change process. Using our kit will save you hours of time, as well as give you peace of mind.

We want to help you navigate the name change process with ease. Now we want to share what we have learned with you. Use our name change kit and follow the step-by-step instructions and guides.

Easy Name Change

The guide to changing your name after marriage

Contents

Name Change Checklist

		DATE COMPLETE
1	**Marriage Certificate**	
2	**Social Security Card**	
3	**Driver's License**	
4	**Vehicle Title and Registration** (If you own a vehicle)	
5	**Passport**	
6	**Voter Registration** (If applicable)	
7	**U.S. Postal Service** (If applicable)	
8	**Personal Accounts**	

IMPORTANT!
Read Before You Start

You must start your name change with the Social Security Administration (SSA). No matter your reason for changing names, Social Security must be updated first. (Unless you have a Green Card. All government agencies link to your SSA record and will only allow a new name that matches.

Have a Green Card? Before starting you must update the name on your Green Card. Once complete, bring your updated Green Card and foreign passport to your Social Security office to begin your name change.

Changed your name before? When updating your name with the Social Security Administration and with your state DMV (driver's license), you must show a complete name change history that links your birth name to your current name. We recommend presenting your birth certificate and any prior legal name change documents (marriage certificates, divorce decrees, or court orders) to avoid any issues.

Mailing documents - Social Security and Passport applications require you to mail in original documents. If you cannot visit these offices in person, we suggest visiting your nearest post office and mailing it via Certified Mail.

1.Marriage Certificate

Overview

You need your marriage certificate in your physical possession to start your name change.

What do I need to do?

Make sure you have your **original** marriage certificate or **a certified copy** in hand.

What does a marriage certificate look like?

It's an official document issued by the government entity (city/county/state/country) where you were married. A marriage certificate contains details about your wedding and has an official stamp or raised seal.

What is a certified copy?

A certified copy is a duplicate marriage certificate issued by the government office that issued your original marriage certificate. It will also contain an official stamp or raised seal.

How do I obtain a certified copy?

Call the office where you applied for your marriage license and request one. Most offices will be able to mail you one in a few business days.

2.Social Security Card

Overview

You must start your name change with the Social Security Administration (SSA).

What do I need to do?

Submit Form SS-5 (enclosed) and the required documentation to your local Social Security office. (By mail or in person)

Here's how to do it:

1. Complete Form SS-5 by filling in sections 1-18:

Notes:

❏ Section 1: Enter your new name

❏ Section 2: Enter your Social Security number

❏ Section 6: Enter your Ethnicity (optional)

❏ Section 7: Enter your Race (optional)

❏ Section 9-10: Enter your parents' birth names (required). Their Social Security Numbers are not required *(select "Unknown" if you choose to omit them).*

❏ Section 14: Enter today's date

❏ Section 17: Sign (use your new name)

2. Gather the <u>required documentation</u>:

❏ Completed Form SS-5

❏ Your marriage certificate - Must be an original or a certified copy *(photocopies not accepted)*

❏ **One (1) Proof of Identity** - Must be current and original:

- U.S. driver's license
- State-issued non-driver's identification card
- U.S. Passport
- Green Card and foreign passport (Non U.S. citizens only)

3. Mail Form SS-5 and the required documentation to your local SSA office OR visit your local SSA office in-person

❏ You must submit your actual legal name change document and your actual proof of identity document. Photocopies are not accepted.

❏ Find the address for your local SSA office here - ssa.gov/locator (Click 'Locate An Office By Zip')

If possible, we recommend submitting in-person; it's faster and doesn't require you to mail in important documents.

If you submit via mail:

You will receive your new Social Security card in two (2) weeks along with any required documentation you submitted with your application. You do not need to provide return postage.

If you submit in-person:

You will be given a receipt showing proof of your name change with the SSA and any required documentation will be given back to you before you leave. Wait at least 48 hours for your SSA record to update before applying for a new driver's license/ID or U.S. Passport. Take the SSA receipt with you when you apply for an updated driver's license/ID. You will receive your new Social Security card in the mail in two (2) weeks.

3.Driver's License

Overview

Update your driver's license or ID card with your new name.

What do I need to do?

Your State requires you to update your license at the Motor Vehicles office. Check your State's website to see if this must be done in person, online, or in person and online

If possible, we recommend updating your driver's license and title/registration at the same time.

We recommend upgrading your standard driver's license to a REAL ID if you haven't already. Starting May 3, 2023, every air traveler will need to present a REAL ID-compliant license or another acceptable form of identification for domestic air travel.

Here's how to update your driver's license/ID:

1. Wait at least 72 hours after changing your name with the Social Security Administration before updating your driver's license.

2. Fill out your State's Driver's license application/update form. Find this at your State's Motor Vehicles website or office

3. If necessary, visit Motor Vehicles office and bring the required documentation. Book an appointment online to avoid the wait if possible

❑ Original or certified copy of your marriage certificate

❑ Your current driver's license/ID card

❑ Your valid U.S. Passport (previous or new name) or U.S. Birth Certificate

❑ Your Social Security card (previous or new name) (If you applied in person and have not received your new card, make sure you bring the receipt you received at the SSA office)

❏ **Two** proofs of [State] residency from **two** separate sources. Must include your residential address and be dated within 60 days (i.e.; utility bill, cable bill, voter registration card).

Make sure your documents are originals. Faxed, photocopied, electronic or laminated copies of documents will not be accepted.

4.Vehicle Title & Registration

Overview

You will need to update your title and registration with your new name if you own a vehicle.

What do I need to do?

Your State requires you to update your registration at the Motor Vehicles office. Check to see if this process is available online. If not, you will have to visit in person.

If possible, we recommend updating your license and title/registration at the same time.

How to update your vehicle title and registration:

1. If your vehicle is leased or financed (lienholder is holding your title), you will have to ask your lienholder to submit the forms to the State Motor Vehicles office

2. Visit a Motor Vehicles office with the required documentation:

[❏ Completed copy of the Vehicle Title and Registration form below]

❏ Original or certified copy of your marriage certificate

❏ Your new driver's license (update your license first)

❏ The title and registration to your vehicle
❏ Proof of liability insurance
❏ Your vehicle (A VIN inspection may be required)

3. The Motor Vehicles office will issue you a new certificate of title and registration card.

4. You may be required to pay applicable title and registration fees.

5.New Passport Application

Overview

You will need to apply for a new passport with your new name.

What do I need to do?

Visit a local passport office or submit an application by mail. (Passport forms are enclosed)

Submit Form DS-11 (*used for first-time applicants, if your current passport was issued when you were under 16 years old, expired passports issued more than 15 years ago, and to replace a lost or damaged passport.*)

OR

Submit Form *DS-82 (If your passport is current or has been expired for less than 5 years)*

OR

Submit *DS-5504 (If your passport was issued less than one year ago)*

Here's how to get a new passport:

1. Complete Form DS-XX:
Notes:
- ❏ Top Section: Select U.S. Passport Book
- ❏ Section 5: Enter your Social Security Number
- ❏ Section 9: Enter your previous name
- ❏ Below Section 9: Staple your passport photo in the square provided. Use four staples vertically, one in each corner, as indicated in the document.
- ❏ Signature Box on Page 1: **Leave blank if indicated by the form.** An agent will need to see you sign and date at the acceptance facility.

2. Gather the required documents:
- ❏ Form DS-XX
- ❏ Color passport photo (as stapled to the form)
- ❏ Proof of U.S. Citizenship: A certified birth certificate. If you were born outside the U.S. you can submit a Certificate of Naturalization, Certificate of Citizenship, Consular Report of Birth Abroad
- ❏ Proof of Identity:

- A valid state-issued driver's license/ID; Certificate of Naturalization; Certificate of Citizenship; military identification; or federal, state, or municipal government employee identification card.
- Your original or certified marriage certificate

3. Submit your application in person/mail (depending on form you selected):

Form DS-11: You must schedule an appointment at a passport acceptance facility either online or by phone. Walk-ins will be turned away. Visit iafdb.travel.state.gov to schedule an appointment at a location near you.

Form DS-82 or Form DS-5504: You may have the options of mailing your application to the address listed on the form

You will be required to pay a $110 application fee (payable to the U.S. State Department) and a $35 execution fee (payable to the acceptance facility)

Next Steps

Your passport will arrive in the mail. Visit passportstatus.state.gov to track the status.

Get a passport picture at the same passport acceptance facility where you apply for your passport. Check iafdb.travel.state.gov to make sure your acceptance facility has photo processing on-site.

6.Voter Registration

Overview

We recommend updating your Voter Registration information.

What do I need to do?

Submit a Voter Registration Application by mail, which
- Registers you to vote in your State
- Updates your name change at your voter registration office
- Updates your address at your voter registration office

How to update your voter registration

1. Complete the Voter Registration Application form (enclosed)
    Notes:

    ❏ Section 6: Enter your driver's license or state ID number. If you don't have one, provide the last 4 digits of your social security number. If you have neither, please write "NONE" on the form.

    ❏ Section 7: Optional but you must register with a party if you want to take part in that party's primary election, caucus, or convention.

    ❏ Section 8: Leave blank

    ❏ Section 9: Sign (use your new/married name) and date

    ❏ Section A: Enter your former name

2. Place the following items in an envelope:

    ❏ Your completed voter registration application

    ❏ A photocopy of your marriage certificate

3. Mail to:

    Address of State Voter Registration Office

7.U.S. Postal Service

This is an OPTIONAL step.

Overview

If you have moved addresses, it's important to keep your address up-to-date with the United States Postal Service (USPS). If you haven't moved, you don't need to update your name or address with the USPS and can skip the rest of this page.

What do I need to do?

Provide USPS your updated name and address at a local post office or online

How to update your address with the USPS:

1. There are two options to update your address

   Option 1 - Visit moversguide.usps.com
   - Use your new name when filling out the form
   - The cost is $1

   Option 2 - Visit your local post office
   - Request a Mover's Guide packet
   - Fill out the form and submit it in the office
   - Use your new name when filling out the form
   - This is free

2. You will receive a confirmation letter at your new address

8. Personal Accounts

Update your personal accounts with your new information

		DATE COMPLETE
1	**Job/Work Information**	
2	**Bank Accounts and Investment Accounts**	
3	**Credit Cards**	
4	**Mortgage/Lease**	
5	**Insurance Policies** Health, Life, Dental, Disability, Car, Homeowner's/Rental, etc.	
6	**Trusted Traveler Programs** Global Entry and TSA PreCheck	
7	**Loyalty Programs** Airlines, Hotels, Retail	
8	**Utilities** Electric, Gas, Water, Garbage, etc.	
9	**Cell Phone**	
10	**TV/Internet**	
11	**Subscriptions** Amazon Prime, Hulu, Netflix, Spotify, etc.	
12	**Email Addresses and Social Media** Gmail, Outlook, Yahoo Mail, Facebook, Tik Tok	

8.1 Personal Accounts: List of Companies

Company	Category	Instructions
AAA	Insurance	1. Call your local member services office or your agent to request a name change 2. Find your nearest office phone number at www.aaa.com
AT&T	Subscriptions	1. Call AT&T customer service: Wireless: (800) 331-0500 Internet or TV: (800) 288-2020 Website: https://www.att.com/support/contact-us/ 2. After verifying your account info, an AT&T customer service agent will be able to update the name on your account 3. You may be asked to provide a copy of your updated photo ID and legal name change document (marriage certificate)
Affirm	Banks	1. Contact Affirm customer care at 855-423-3729 or https://helpcenter.affirm.com/s/contact-us and request a name change on your account 2. A customer care agent will update the name on your account after verifying your identity over the phone 3. Note, you may be to submit supporting documentation of your name change such as a copy of your updated photo ID and a copy of your legal name change document (marriage certificate)
Afterpay	Banks	1. Send an email to info@afterpay.com (subject line: 'Name Change Request') and request a name change on your account; or Contact customer support at (855) 289-6014 2. A customer support agent will email you a name change form to complete and return along with a copy of your updated photo ID (driver's license or passport)
Airbnb	Travel Loyalty	1. Sign into your Airbnb account - airbnb.com 2. Click on your profile picture in the upper-right-hand corner and select 'Account' > 'Personal Info' 3. Update your legal name and select 'Save'.
Amazon Rewards Visa (Chase)	Credit Cards	1. Contact Chase Bank customer service at 1-888-247-4080 online at: https://www.chase.com/digital/customer-service or the number on the back of the card 2. Let a customer support agent know about your name change 3. You may need to provide a copy of your updated ID and legal name change document (marriage certificate)
Amazon Store Card	Credit Cards	1. Contact Customer Service at 1-844-406-7321 or the number on the back of your card 2. You will be asked to enter your account number 3. A customer service agent will be able to update your name over the phone
American Airlines AAdvantage	Travel Loyalty	1. Log into your AAdvantage account - aa.com 2. Visit aa.com/contact/forms 3. Select Topic > AAdvantage Account Service, Subject > Name / Address Change 4. Upload a copy of your updated photo ID (driver's license or passport) and a copy of your legal name change document

		(marriage certificate) OR Phone: 1. Contact AAdvantage customer service at 800-882-8880 2. Tell the customer service rep that you'd like to change your name and they'll send you an email with instructions 3. Reply to the email with a copy of your updated photo ID (driver's license or passport) and a copy of your legal name change document (marriage certificate)
American Express	Credit Cards	1. Log on to www.americanexpress.com 2. Search for the name change authorization form. Complete the form and upload your new State ID or Passport
Apple Card	Credit Cards	1. Open Wallet on your iPhone and tap Apple Card 2. Tap the more button, then tap the Message button to start chatting with an Apple Card Specialist 3. Request to change the name on your account
Apple ID and iCloud	Subscriptions	1. Sign into your account - appleid.apple.com 2. In the Account section, click Edit 3. Under your Apple ID, click Change Apple ID to match your new email address (if applicable). If you try to change your Apple ID to an @icloud.com email address created within the last 30 days, you might be asked to try again later. 4. Under Payment & Shipping, click Edit to enter your update payment info and shipping info (if applicable)
Apple TV	Subscriptions	1. Log into your account at tv.apple.com 2. Click on the profile icon at the top right and select "Settings" 3. On the Account Settings page click "Edit" under "Account Summary" 4. You will be taken to the Apple ID page. Log into your Apple account here. 5. Under "Account" click on "Edit" 6. Update your name, then click "Done"
BMO Harris Bank	Banks	1. Find the nearest BMO Harris Bank branch location: branchlocator.bmoharris.com/ 2. Schedule an appointment if your location permits ('Book an appointment') 3. Bring your updated photo ID and legal name change document (marriage certificate) to the branch 4. BMO Harris Bank will update your account and document your new signature 5. If you're unable to visit a branch location contact customer service at 1-888- 340-2265
Bank of America	Banks	To update your checking, savings,or credit card: 1. Locate your nearest Bank of America financial center: locators.bankofamerica.com 2. Schedule an appointment if your location permits ('Schedule an appointment') 3. Bring your photo ID (new or old name) and legal name change document (marriage certificate) 4. An associate will give you forms to complete 5. If you're unable to visit a financial center contact customer service at 800-432- 1000 and request a name change

Easy Name Change

The guide to changing your name after marriage

Bank of America Credit Card	Credit Cards	To update a Bank of America credit card: 1. Locate your nearest Bank of America financial center: locators.bankofamerica.com 2. Bring your photo ID (new or old name) and legal name change document (marriage certificate, divorce decree or court order) to any Bank of America financial center 3. An associate will give you forms to complete and will assist you with obtaining a new credit card 4. If you're unable to visit a financial center contact customer service at 800-432- 1000
Barclays	Credit Cards	To update your name on your Barclays credit card(s) you need to mail in a name change request 1. On a blank sheet of paper, write 'Change of Name Request', your new name, your old name, and the last four digits of your card number(s) 2. Include a photocopy of your updated photo ID (driver's license or passport) and a photocopy of your legal name change document (marriage certificate) 3. Mail to: Attn: Customer Card Correspondence P.O. Box 8801 Wilmington, DE 19899 The correspondence team will respond upon the receipt of the documentation within two days, and a replacement card will be mailed to you
Best Buy	Credit Cards	My Best Buy Credit Card, My Best Buy Visa Card and My Best Buy MasterCard: 1. Contact Citibank (issuer) customer service at 1-888-574-1301 or the number on the back of the card 2. You may need to provide a copy of your updated photo ID and legal name change document (marriage certificate)
Best Western Rewards	Travel Loyalty	1. Contact Best Western Rewards customer service at 1-800-237-8483 or https://www.bestwestern.com/en_US/customer-service/bwr-customer-service.html 2. A customer service rep will be able to update your name over the phone
Bloomingdale's	Credit Cards	Bloomingdale's Credit Card and/or your Bloomingdale's American Express Card 1. Contact Customer Service at 1-888-257-6762 2. A customer service agent will be able to update your name over the phone after verifying your information Online: 1. Log into your Bloomindale's account - bloomingdales.com (select 'My Account') 2. Select the 'Credit summary' link under the "My Bloomingdale's Credit Card" section 3. Scroll down to the footer of the page and select 'Send Secure Message' 4. Include your new name, old name and reason for your name change
Blue Cross Blue Shield (BCBS)	Insurance	Employer-sponsored Plans: Contact your HR department or your plan's administrator and request a member change form. Individual & Family Plans: Contact the number on the back of

Easy Name Change

The guide to changing your name after marriage

		your member ID card. A member service representative will provide you with the proper member change form.
Blue Cross Blue Shield of Massachusetts	Insurance	Employee-Sponsored Plans: Contact your HR department or your benefits administrator and request a name change. Name change requests must be made through your employer. If you purchased your plan directly from Blue Cross Blue Shield of Massachusetts: Request a name change on your policy by Contacting the phone number on the back of your Member ID card or 1-800-262-2583. Depending on the type of plan(s) you have, a member service representative may be able to update your name over the phone. If not, a member service representative will provide you with the proper member change form for your plan type(s).
Blue Shield of California	Insurance	Employer-sponsored Plans: Contact your HR department or your plan's administrator and request a name change. Name change requests must be made through your employer. Individual & Family Plans: Contact (800) 393-6130 or the number on the back of your member ID card. After verifying your information over the phone, a member services representative will place a name change request on your account. You may be required to complete a policy change form depending on the type of policy or policies you have. Policy change forms are not available online. If you purchased your plan through the Healthcare.gov Marketplace: You can update your policy via the Healthcare.gov Marketplace by phone (800-318- 2596) or online (see instructions below): 1. Log into your HealthCare.gov account. 2. Choose the application you want to update. 3. Click "Report a Life Change" on the left-hand menu. 4. Read through the list of changes, and click "Report a Life Change" to get started.
Booking.com	Travel Loyalty	1. Log into your Booking.com account - booking.com 2. Click on your name in the top navigation menu and then select Settings 3. Under For When You Book, update your name
CIBC U.S.	Banks	You can update your name via mail, fax, or by visiting any CIBC U.S. Banking Center. Banking Center: 1. Bring your updated driver's license and your legal name change document (marriage certificate) to any CIBC Banking Center location 2. A CIBC customer service representative will update your account and document your new signature
CVS Caremark	Insurance	Contact your HR department or your health plan's administrator and request a name change on your account.
Capital One Bank	Banks	You must mail or fax in supporting documentation of your name change. 1. On a blank sheet of paper, write 'Change of Name Request', your new name, your old name, your account number, today's date, and your signature (in your new name). 2. Fill out and sign a W-9 form (Request for Taxpayer

		Identification Number and Certification Form) to match the name changes you want to make - irs.gov/pub/irs-pdf/fw9.pdf 3. Mail or fax the written request, completed W-9, a photocopy of your updated photo ID (driver's license or passport), and a photocopy of your legal name change document (marriage certificate) to: Mail: Capital One P.O. Box 60 St. Cloud, MN 56302 Fax: 877-464-4963 (attn: Capital One) It takes about 3 business days to process your name change
Capital One Credit Card	Credit Cards	1. Contact Capital One credit card customer service at 1-888-464-0727 and they will be able to process your name change over the phone 2. You may need to provide a copy of your updated photo ID and legal name change document (marriage certificate)
Charles Schwab	Investments	1. Complete the Schwab Name Change Form 2. Submit the completed form and a copy of your legal name change document (marriage certificate) Online: Sign into your Schwab account and click the Message Center link (under Accounts). Click the Compose New Message link and upload the completed form and a copy of your legal name change document. Mail: Charles Schwab & Co., Inc. P.O. Box 982600 El Paso, TX 79998-2600
Charles Schwab Bank	Banks	1. Complete the Schwab Name Change Form 2. Submit the completed form and a copy of your legal name change document (marriage certificate) Online: Sign into your Schwab account and click the Message Center link (under Accounts). Click the Compose New Message link and upload the completed form and a copy of your legal name change document. Mail: Charles Schwab & Co., Inc. P.O. Box 982600 El Paso, TX 79998-2600
Chase Bank	Banks	1. Locate your nearest Chase Bank branch: locator.chase.com 2. Contact your branch ahead of time to schedule an appointment if your location is frequently busy 3. Bring your updated photo ID and legal name change document (marriage certificate) to the nearest Chase Bank branch 4. Chase Bank will update your account and document your new signature 5. If you're unable to visit a branch location contact customer service at 1-800- 935-9935
Chase Credit Card	Credit Cards	1. Contact customer service at the number on the back of your card or 1-800-432- 3117 (available 24/7). 2. Enter your account information and select "0" to speak with

		a customer support agent. 3. Tell the customer service agent your legal name has changed. 4. The customer service agent will submit your change request and you will be mailed a name change packet. 5. Mail or fax the completed name change packet back to Chase. Note, you may be required to include a copy of your updated photo ID and a copy of your legal name change document (marriage certificate). 6. Once the packet is received, you will be mailed a new card for each account you have open.
Chevron	Credit Cards	Techron Advantage Card: 1. Contact Customer Service at (844) 442-7932 or the number on the back of your card 2. You will be asked to enter your account number 3. A customer service agent will be able to update your name over the phone
Choice Privileges	Travel Loyalty	You can update your name via email or mail. Email: Send an email to member_documents@choicehotels.com (subject line: Name Change Request). Include your new name, your old name, and the reason for your name change (marriage), and attach a copy of your photo ID (driver's license or passport) showing your old name, a copy of your photo ID (driver's license or passport) showing your new name, and a copy of your legal name change document (marriage certificate). Mail: 1. On a blank sheet of paper, write 'Change of Name Request', your new name, your old name, and the reason for your name change (marriage) 2. Mail your written request letter, a copy of your photo ID (driver's license or passport) showing your old name, a copy of your photo ID (driver's license or passport) showing your new name, and a copy of your legal name change document (marriage certificate) to: Choice Hotels International Member Services Department 6811 E. Mayo Boulevard, Ste. 100 Phoenix, AZ 85054
Chubb	Insurance	1. Contact your Chubb agent/broker and request a name change on your policy (policy changes must be completed by your agent) 2. You can find your agent's contact info by Contacting 866-324-8222 (option #2) or visiting chubb.com/us-en/individuals-families/find-an-agent 3. After verifying your identity over the phone, your agent may ask you to submit supporting documentation such as an updated photo ID and/or legal name change document (marriage certificate, divorce decree or court order) before updating your policy
Citi	Banks	To update a Citi checking or savings account: 1. Locate your nearest Citi branch: https://online.citi.com/US/ag/citibank-location finder.

		2. Contact your branch ahead of time to schedule an appointment if your location is frequently busy 3. Bring your updated photo ID and legal name change document (marriage certificate) to the nearest Citi branch 4. Citi will update your account and document your new signature
Citi Credit Card	Credit Cards	1. Contact Citi customer service at the number on the back of your card or 1-800- 950-5114 2. A customer service agent will be able to make the update over the phone 3. Depending on the type of card(s) you have, you may need to provide a copy of your updated ID and legal name change document (marriage certificate)
Citizens Bank	Banks	To update a Citizens checking account, savings account, de card, credit card, loan, or credit line: 1. Bring your updated photo ID and legal name change document (marriage certificate) to the nearest Citizens Bank branch. 2. Citizens Bank will update your account after you sign an updated signature card 3. To find the nearest location visit citizensbank.com/customer-service/branch locator.aspx 4. If you are unable to visit a branch location, Contact customer service at 1-800-922- 9999 or visit https://www.citizensbank.com/customer-service/contact-us.asp
Comcast	Subscriptions	Take your government issued ID (showing your married name) to your local Comast Service Center location
Costco	Subscriptions	Bring an updated photo ID (driver's license or passport) to the Member Services desk
Costco Anywhere Visa Card by Citi	Credit Cards	1. Contact Citi Customer Service at 1-855-378-6467 or the number on the back of your card 2. Enter your credit card number over the phone 3. Ask to speak to a customer service agent 4. A customer service agent will be able to update your name over the phone
Delta SkyMiles	Travel Loyalty	1. Log in to your SkyMiles account - delta.com OR 2. Contact customer service at: 1-800-323-2323
Discover	Credit Cards	1. Log into your Discover account - discover.com 2. Click Inbox or Secure Document Center to send a secure email message 3. Upload a copy of your updated photo ID (driver's license or passport) or your legal name change document (marriage certificate) - a photo from your cell phone will work as long as the picture includes all four corners and is legible 4. In the subject line type 'CHANGE OF NAME' 5. In the description type 'Name change due to marriage' 6. Discover will send you an email notifying you when the name change is complete 7. If you have additional questions contact customer service at 1-800-347-2683 or visit: https://www.discover.com/credit-cards/help-center/faqs/web-support.html

Dish	Subscriptions	You can update your name via phone or live chat: Phone: 1. Contact DISH account services at (866) 974-0769 2. Tell the account services agent that your legal name has changed and request a name change on your account 3. The account services agent will provide you with a link to upload supporting documentation of your name change Live Chat: 1. Sign into your dish account - dish.com 2. Once signed in, under Contact Us click the 'Live Chat' or 'Chat With Us' button to connect with customer support 3. Tell the customer support agent that your legal name has changed and request a name change on your account 4. The customer support agent will provide you with a link to upload supporting documentation of your name change
Disney+	Subscriptions	1. Go to disneyplus.com 2. Click on your Profile in top right corner 3. Click on Account 4. Click Billing Details, then Update payment info 5. Update with your new payment information 6. Click Save. This will save your updated payment information to your Disney+ account
E*Trade	Investments	1. Log into your E*TRADE account - etrade.com 2. Visit the Forms and Applications page 3. Find the Name Change Authorization Form and select Submit Online 4. Complete the form and upload a copy of your legal name change document (marriage certificate)
Edward Jones	Investments	1. You must contact your Financial Advisor to update your last name 2. To find your Finacial Advisor visit edwardjones.com
EmblemHealth	Insurance	Employer-sponsored Plans: Contact your HR department or your plan's administrator and request a name change. Name change requests must be made through your employer. If you purchased your plan through the New York State of Health: Contact the New York State of Health contact center at 1-855-355-5777. A representative will be able to update your policy after verifying your identity over the phone. If you purchased your plan through the Healthcare.gov Marketplace: You can update your policy by phone 800-318-2596 or online (see instructions below): 1. Log into your HealthCare.gov account. 2. Choose the application you want to update. 3. Click "Report a Life Change" on the left-hand menu. 4. Read through the list of changes, and click "Report a Life Change" to get started. 5. Select the kind of change you want to report (marriage)
Expedia	Travel Loyalty	1. Log into your Expedia account - expedia.com 2. Under My Account, click Personal Info 3. Update your name and click Save
Fidelity	Investments	Individual Accounts: 1. You can update your name online by visiting fidelity.com/customer service/how-to-update-name

		2. On the Name Change page, enter your new name 3. Attach a copy of your legal name change document (marriage certificate) and submit the request Employer-sponsored Accounts: If you have a 401(k) or another type of a workplace account, request a name change with your employer or log into your NetBenefits account to make the update.
Fidelity & Guaranty Life	Insurance	1. Complete the Request for Service Form - fglife.com/contact/manage policies/how-to-change-name.html 2. Mail the completed form and a copy of your updated photo ID (driver's license or passport) or a copy of your legal name change document (marriage certificate) to: the address on the form
Fidelity Rewards	Credit Cards	1. Contact Cardmember Service at 888-551-5144 or the number on the back of your card and request a name change on your account 2. A customer service agent will mail you a name change form to complete (the form is only available by request) 3. Mail the completed name change form, a copy of your updated photo ID (driver's license or passport), and a copy of your legal name change document (marriage certificate)
Gap	Credit Cards	Gap Visa Card or Gap Card: 1. Contact Customer Service at 1-855-605-4360 or the number on the back of your card 2. A customer service agent will be able to update your name over the phone
GEICO	Insurance	1. Log into your Geico account - geico.com 2. Under My Account, click Edit Profile, update your name, and click save.
Gmail	Email	1. Log into your account. Click the gear icon at the top right of the screen and select "Mail Settings". 2. In the "Send Mail As" section, click edit. Enter your new name. Click Save
Global Entry	Travel Programs	1. Contact your nearest Global Entry Enrollment Center 2. Ask an officer and ask if they can process your name change request over the phone. If not, you will need to show up in person. No appointment is needed. 3. Bring your Global Entry card, new passport, and your legal name change document (marriage certificate) to a Global Entry Enrollment Center. 4. Present your documents to an officer to update your name. Note: Updating your Global Entry membership will also update your TSA PreCheck membership. If you have both Trusted Traveler Programs, updating Global Entry first will save you an extra step. Tip: If your enrollment center is at an airport, save an extra trip by arriving a few hours early before your next flight and updating your name then (appointment not required).
Goldman Sachs 401k	Investments	Goldman Sachs 401k (managed by HR Workways) 1. Contact 1-877-454-7426 (toll-free) or 1-847-883-1048. 2. Tell a representative that your legal name has changed and they will provide you with instructions on how to upload

		supporting documentation required to process your name change request
HSBC Bank	Banks	1. Bring your updated photo ID and marriage certificate to the nearest HSBC Bank branch 2. HSBC Bank will update your account and document your new signature 3. To find the nearest location visit https://mapp.us.hsbc.com/1/2/3/branch-locator 4. If you're unable to visit a branch location contact customer service at 1-800-975-4722
Hanover Insurance Group	Insurance	If you purchased your policy directly through Hanover Insurance Group: 1. Contact Customer Support at 508-855-1000 and request a name change on your account/policy. A customer support agent will be able to update your account after verifying your identity. If you are updating your auto policy, you will be required to provide your new driver's license number. 2. If you purchased your policy through an independent insurance agent: Contact your insurance agent and request a name change on your policy. Name changes must be processed by your agent. You can find your agent's contact information on your monthly statement.
Hilton Grand Vacations	Travel Loyalty	1. Send an email to titleservices@hgvc.com (subject line: 'Name Change Request'). 2. Include your new name, your old name, your member ID, and attach a photocopy of your updated photo ID and a photocopy of your legal name change document (marriage certificate). Note, if you currently have a loan on your account you may not be eligible to change the name on your account. An HGV customer service agent will contact you to finalize the account update. Club Member Services: 800-932-4482 or visit: https://www.hiltongrandvacations.com/en/contact-us
Home Depot	Credit Cards	1. Log into your Home Depot credit card account 2. Go to the 'Account Profile' menu at the top of the page, then select 'Edit Contact Information 3. You will need to provide your account number, the reason for your name change, your signature, and supporting documentation 4. If you are not able to complete the request online, contact customer service at 1-866-875-5488 or the number on the back of your card
Hotmail	Email	1. Login to your account. Click the Options link at the top right of the screen. 2. Click on Account details under Manage your account. 3. Locate your name and replace it with your new name.
Hulu	Subscriptions	1. Log into your Hulu account - hulu.com 2. Hover over your name in the top right-hand corner and click Account 3. Next, update your Payment Information and Personal Information
Humana	Insurance	Employer-sponsored Plans: Contact 1-800-448-6262 or the number on the back of your member ID card. After verifying

		your identity over the phone, a customer support agent will be able to update the name on your Humana account. Individual & Family Plans: Contact 1-877-877-1051 or the number on the back of your member ID card. After verifying your identity over the phone, a customer support agent will be able to update the name on your Humana account.
Hyatt	Travel Loyalty	You must mail or fax in supporting documentation of your name change. On a blank sheet of paper, write 'Change of Name Request', your new name, your old name, and your account number. Include a photocopy of your updated photo ID (driver's license or passport) and a photocopy of your legal name change document (marriage certificate) Mail: World of Hyatt Customer Service Center P.O. Box 27089 Omaha, NE 68144 USA Fax: (402) 593-9449 OR visit: https://help.hyatt.com/en.html
IHG Rewards Club	Travel Loyalty	1. Email ihgrewardsclub@ihg.com and include your member number, a copy of your updated photo ID (driver's license or passport), and a copy of your legal name change document (marriage certificate) 2. You will receive an auto-reply from the IHG email support team and you should receive a confirmation email after the update has been made 3. If you experience any difficulties, contact the IHG Rewards Club Customer Care Center at 888-695-4678 or visit: https://www.ihg.com/content/us/en/customer-care/main
Instacart	Subscriptions	Via the Instacart app: 1. Tap View account under your name at the top of the app dashboard or the three stacked horizontal lines in the upper left corner 2. Tap Your account settings 3. Tap Your name, email, and phone 4. Update the information you'd like to change and tap Save Via the Instacart website: 1. At the top right, click "Account" 2. Click Your Account and click Change next to the information you'd like to update 3. Update the information and click Save
J.Crew	Credit Cards	1. Contact J.Crew customer service at 1-888-428-8810 or call the number on the back of your card 2. Verify your identity over the phone and request to speak to customer service
John Hancock	Investments	1. Complete the Name Change Form - jhinvestments.com/resources/all resources/forms-and-applications/name-change-form 2. Mail the completed form to: John Hancock Signature Services, Inc.

		P.O. Box 219909 Kansas City, MO 64121-9909
Kohl's Credit Card	credit Cards	Contact customer service at 855-564-5748 or the number on the back of your card. A new credit card will be mailed to you in your new name
LendingClub	Banks	1. Visit www.lendingclub.com 2. Enter your email address linked to your account and select My Account > Account Status 3. In the Subject line type 'Name Change' and then select Continue 4. Enter your Loan ID and a short description (i.e. "my legal name changed and I'd like to update my account") 5. Attach a copy of your updated photo ID (driver's license or passport) and a copy of your legal name change document (marriage certificate) Visit: https://help.lendingclub.com/hc/en-us/articles/215562677-Changing-your profile-information#legal
Liberty Mutual	Insurance	Contact 1-844-629-8984 and a customer support representative can process your name change over the phone after verifying your identity and policy number(s).
Lowe's	Credit Cards	Lowe's Advantage Card and Lowe's Visa Rewards: 1. Contact Customer Service at 1-888-840-7651 or the number on the back of your card 2. You will be asked to enter your account number 3. A customer service agent will be able to update your name over the phone
Macys	Credit Cards	Macy's Store Credit Card or Macy's American Express® Card: Option 1 -> Contact Customer Service at 1-888-257-6757 or the number on the back of your card Option 2 -> Send a secure message 1. Log in to your Macy's account with your email address and password 2. Select "credit summary" under "my Macy's Credit Card" 3. Scroll down to the footer of the page and select "Send Secure Message" 4. Let the customer support agent know about your name change You may need to provide a copy of your updated ID and legal name change document (marriage certificate)
MetLife (Home and Auto)	Insurance	1. Send an email to policyupdate@metlife.com (subject line: 'Name Change Request'). 2. Include your old name, your new name, the reason for your name change (marriage), and attach a copy of your updated photo ID (driver's license or passport), and a copy of your legal name change document (marriage certificate). 3. A customer support agent will respond and process your name change request.
Millennium Trust Company	Investments	You must email or fax in supporting documentation of your name change. 1. On a blank sheet of paper, write 'Change of Name Request', your new name, your old name, the reason for your name change, today's date, and your signature (in your new

		name)
		2. Submit the written request letter, a copy of your updated photo ID (driver's license or passport), and a copy of your legal name change document (marriage certificate) Email: Scan and send to arp@mtrustcompany.com (subject line 'Name Change Request')
Mint (Intuit)	Investments	1. Log into your Mint.com account - mint.intuit.com 2. In the top navigation bar, select 'Profile' and proceed to update your name
Morgan Stanley	Investments	1. Contact your Morgan Stanley financial advisor (advisor search - advisor.morganstanley.com/search) 2. Tell your financial advisor that your legal name has changed 3. Your financial advisor will verify your identity over the phone and then proceed to update your account information 4. If you can't find your financial advisor's contact information, Contact Morgan Stanley customer support at 1-888-454-3965 and a support agent will be able to provide you with it
Navy Federal Credit Union	Banks	Log onto www.navyfederal.org, complete the online name change form and submit it with the scanned copy of your marriage certificate. If you have questions call customer service at 888-842-6328
Netflix	Subscriptions	1. Log into your account at netflix.com to update your Netflix account information 2. If you are being billed through a third party and not directly through Netflix, please visit the third party's website to update your information
NEXUS	Travel Programs	1. Contact your nearest NEXUS Enrollment Center 2. Speak to an officer and ask if they can process your name change request over the phone. If not, you will need to show up in person. No appointment is needed. 3. Bring your NEXUS card, your updated passport, your updated driver's license, and your legal name change document (marriage certificate) 4. Present your documents to an officer to update your name. https://www.cbp.gov/travel/trusted-traveler-programs/nexus/enrollment-centers
Nationwide	Insurance	Online: 1. Log into your Nationwide account - nationwide.com 2. Once logged in, select Contact Us and select 'Send us an email' 3. Complete the online form and place a written name change request in the message box. Include your old name, your new name, and the reason for your name change (marriage). Nationwide will contact you if they require supporting documentation of your name change Phone: 1. Contact Nationwide customer support at 1-877-669-6877 (have your account # or policy # ready) 2. After verifying your identity over the phone, a customer support agent will be able to update the name on your account and policies

Easy Name Change

The guide to changing your name after marriage

Nordstrom	Credit Cards	Nordstrom Platinum Visa and Nordstrom Retail credit card: Contact 1-800-964- 1800 or the number on the back of your card Nordstrom Visa Signature: Contact 1-866-445-0433 or the number on the back of your card Nordstrom de card: Contact 1-866-445-0426 or the number on the back of your card A Customer Service agent will be able to update your name over the phone
PNC Bank Credit Card	Credit Cards	1. Contact PNC Bank customer service at 1-888-762-2265 or the number on the back of your card 2. Tell a customer service agent that your legal name has changed 3. The agent will update the name on your account over the phone
PayPal Mastercard	Credit Cards	1. Contact Customer Service at 866-657-5788 or the number on the back of your card 2. A customer service agent will be able to update your name over the phone
Planters Bank	Banks	1. Bring your your updated photo ID (driver's license or passport), and your legal name change document (marriage certificate) to any Planters Bank branch location - plantersbankonline.com/locations.aspx 2. A representative will update your account and document your new signature 3. If you're unable to visit a branch location contact Planters Bank customer support at 888-806-7036
Prudential Financial	Investments	Employer-sponsored Investment Accounts: If you are currently enrolled through your employer, notify your HR department or your benefit plan administrator and request a name change. Name change requests must be made through your employer. Individual Investment Accounts (Mutual Funds, Traditional IRA, Roth IRA, SEP IRA, Coverdell ESA and 403(b)): 1. Complete the Name Change Form (MF 1003) 2. Mail the completed form and a copy of your legal name change document (marriage certificate): Prudential Mutual Fund Services LLC P.O. Box 9658 Providence, RI 02940
Quicken Loans	Banks	1. Contact Quicken Loans mortgage services at 800-508-0944 2. You will be asked to verify your identity over the phone 3. Tell a customer support agent that your legal name has changed 4. You will be given instructions on how to submit supporting documentation (such as a copy of your updated driver's license or passport) via fax, mail, or email
Raymond James	Investments	1. Reach out to your financial advisor or nearest branch office - raymondjames.com 2. Tell your financial advisor that your legal name has

		changed 3. Your financial advisor will send you the proper name change form based on your account type(s) 4. You will be required to return the name change form along with any required supporting documentation
Revolut	Credit Cards	1. Open the Revolut app on your phone 2. Once logged in, go to "Dashboard" and "?" to start a "New chat" 3. Request a name change on your account 4. A customer service specialist will be able to update your name after verifying your identity
Robinhood	Investments	1. Send an email to support@robinhood.com 2. In the subject line put 'Requesting Name Change' 3. Robinhood will send you an email back with instructions on how to update your and along with a secure file submission link for you to upload your documents 4. Using the secure file submission link, upload a photo of your legal name change document (marriage certificate), an updated photo ID with your preferred name and a signed letter of authorization from you requesting the name change on your Robinhood account
Roku	Subscriptions	1. Log into your account at roku.com 2. Click on the profile icon in the upper right and select "My Account" 3. Under "Account information" click "Update" 4. Update your name
Sam's Club Credit Card	Credit Cards	1. Contact Customer Service at 1-800-964-1917 or the number on the back of your card 2. You will be asked to enter your account number 3. A customer service agent will be able to update your name over the phone
Sephora	Credit Cards	1. Contact Sephora customer service: Sephora Credit Card or Sephora Visa: 1-866-841-5037 Sephora Visa Signature: 1-866-864-7787 2. Verify your identity over the phone 3. A customer service agent will be able to make the update over the phone
State Farm Insurance	Insurance	Contact you local agent and they will update the name on your policy
Spotify	Subscriptions	1. Log into your account at spotify.com 2. Select Subscription in the menu on the left 3. Under Payment method, click UPDATE 4. Choose your payment method at the top and fill in the details 5. Click CHANGE PAYMENT DETAILS to confirm.
Sprint	Subscriptions	1. You can complete your name change online by visiting https://sprint.com/global/pdf/support/Sprint-change-billing-name-form.pdf 2. Follow the instructions and you will be asked to upload your legal name change document (marriage certificate) OR visit your nearest Sprintstore with your legal name change document

Starbucks	Store Loyalty	1. Log into your account at starbucks.com and click "My Account" 2. Select "Settings" 3. Update your name in the Personal Info section and click "Save"
Sunoco	Credit Cards	1. Contact Sunoco Credit Card customer service at 1-866-622-3574 or the number on the back of your card 2. Enter your account number over the phone 3. Request a name change on your account 4. A customer service agent will be able to update your name over the phone
T-Mobile	Subscriptions	1. Visit a local T-Mobile retail location 2. Bring along your updated photo ID (driver's license or passport) and your legal name change document (marriage certificate) 3. To locate your nearest store visit t-mobile.com/store-locator
TD Ameritrade	Investments	1. Complete the Name Change Authorization https://www.tdameritrade.com/retail-en_us/resources/pdf/TDA2333.pdf 2. Submit the completed form and a copy of your legal name change document (marriage certificate) by mail or a secure message: Mail: TD Ameritrade PO Box 2760 Omaha, NE 68103-2760 Secure Message: 1. Log into your TD Ameritrade account 2. Access the Secure Message Center by clicking the bell icon 3. Upload your documents and click Send
TD Bank	Banks	1. Bring your updated photo ID and legal name change document (marriage certificate) to a TD Bank branch 2. TD Bank will update your account and document your new signature 3. If you're unable to visit a branch location contact customer service at 1-888-751-9000
TD Retail Card Services	Credit Cards	1. Contact TD Retail Card Services at 800-252-2551 or the number of the back of your card 2. A customer service agent will email or mail you a name change form to complete 3. Return the completed form back to TD Retail Card Services along with a copy of your updated photo ID (driver's license or passport)
TJ Maxx (TJX)	Credit Cards	1. Contact Customer Service: TJX Rewards Credit Card: 1-800-952-6133 or the number on the back of your card TJX Rewards Platinum MasterCard: 1-877-890-3150 or the number on the back of your card 2. You will be asked to enter your account number 3. A customer service agent will be able to update your name over the phone

Easy Name Change

The guide to changing your name after marriage

TSA Pre	Travel Programs	1. Contact customer service at: 855-347-8371 2. Speak to an agent and request a name change 3. An agent will ask you to email or fax a copy of your legal name change document (marriage certificate), photo ID (updated passport with your new name OR both sides of an updated photo ID), known traveler number, and an identifier they give you over the phone
Target REDcard	Credit Cards	1. Contact Target Customer Care: Target Mastercard: 1-800-424-6888 or the number on the back of your card Target Credit Card: 1-800-659-2396 or the number on the back of your card 2. A customer care associate will be able to update your name over the phone
USAA Federal Savings Bank	Banks	Contact 800-531-8722 and a bank representative will assist you over the phone
US Bank	Banks	1. Locate your nearest US Bank branch: locations.usbank.com/search.html 2. Bring your updated photo ID and legal name change document (marriage certificate) to a US Bank branch 3. If you're unable to visit a branch location contact customer service at 800-872- 2657 or visit https://www.usbank.com/customer-service.html
Venmo	Banks	1. Open the Venmo app on your phone 2. Tap the drop-down navigation icon in the upper-left 3. Tap "Settings", then tap "Edit Profile" 4. Update your name and tap "Save"
Venmo De Card	Banks	1. Open a support ticket with Venmo - help.venmo.com/hc/en-us/requests/new 2. Fill out the form and select 'Venmo De Credit Question' 3. Upload a copy of your updated photo ID (driver's license or passport) and a copy of your legal name change document (marriage certificate) 4. You will receive a confirmation email from a Venmo customer support agent confirming your name change
Verizon	Subscriptions	1. Contact Verizon customer support at 1-800-VERIZON (1-800-837-4966) 2. Enter your account info and ask to speak to a customer support representative
Verizon Wireless	Subscriptions	1. Contact Verizon Wireless customer support at 1-800-922-0204 2. Enter your account info and ask to speak to a customer support representative
Victoria's Secret	Credit Cards	1. Contact Victoria's Secret customer service at 1-800-695-9478 2. Verify your identity over the phone and request to speak to customer service 3. A customer service agent will be able to make the update over the phone
Walmart	Credit Cards	1. Contact Customer Service at 1-877-294-7880 or the number on the back of your card 2. You will be asked to enter your account number

		3. A customer service agent will be able to update your name over the phone
Wells Fargo	Banks	1. Locate your nearest Wells Fargo Bank branch: wellsfargo.com/locator 2. Bring your updated photo ID and legal name change document (marriage certificate) to a Wells Fargo Bank branch office 3. If you're unable to visit a branch location contact customer service at 1-800- 869-3557 or visit: https://www.wellsfargo.com/help/
Wells Fargo Home Mortgage	Banks	You must submit a written name change request letter via mail or fax. On a blank sheet of paper, write 'Change of Name Request', your new name, former name, account/loan number, and your signature (in your new name). Send the written request and a photocopy of your legal name change document (marriage certificate) to: Fax: 1-866-278-1179 (ATTN: Written Correspondence) Mail: Wells Fargo Home Mortgage Written Correspondence P.O. Box 10335 Des Moines, IA 50306-0335 If you have any questions contact Wells Fargo Home Mortgage customer service at 1-800-288-3212

Easy Name Change

The guide to changing your name after marriage

Appendix: Social Security Application Form

Application for a Social Security Card

Applying for a Social Security Card is free!

USE THIS APPLICATION TO:

- Apply for an original Social Security card
- Apply for a replacement Social Security card
- Change or correct information on your Social Security number record

IMPORTANT: You MUST provide a properly completed application and the required evidence before we can process your application. We can only accept original documents or documents certified by the custodian of the original record. Notarized copies or photocopies which have not been certified by the custodian of the record are not acceptable. We will return any documents submitted with your application. For assistance call us at 1-800-772-1213 or visit our website at **www.socialsecurity.gov**.

Original Social Security Card

To apply for an original card, you must provide at least two documents to prove age, identity, and U.S. citizenship or current lawful, work-authorized immigration status. If you are not a U.S. citizen and do not have DHS work authorization, you must prove that you have a valid non-work reason for requesting a card. See page 2 for an explanation of acceptable documents.

NOTE: If you are age 12 or older and have never received a Social Security number, you must apply in person.

Replacement Social Security Card

To apply for a replacement card, you must provide one document to prove your identity. If you were born outside the U.S., you must also provide documents to prove your U.S. citizenship or current, lawful, work-authorized status. See page 2 for an explanation of acceptable documents.

Changing Information on Your Social Security Record

To change the information on your Social Security number record (i.e., a name or citizenship change, or corrected date of birth) you must provide documents to prove your identity, support the requested change, and establish the reason for the change. For example, you may provide a birth certificate to show your correct date of birth. A document supporting a name change must be recent and identify you by both your old and new names. If the name change event occurred over two years ago or if the name change document does not have enough information to prove your identity, you must also provide documents to prove your identity in your prior name and/or in some cases your new legal name. If you were born outside the U.S. you must provide a document to prove your U.S. citizenship or current lawful, work-authorized status. See page 2 for an explanation of acceptable documents.

LIMITS ON REPLACEMENT SOCIAL SECURITY CARDS

Public Law 108-458 limits the number of replacement Social Security cards you may receive to 3 per calendar year and 10 in a lifetime. Cards issued to reflect changes to your legal name or changes to a work authorization legend do not count toward these limits. We may also grant exceptions to these limits if you provide evidence from an official source to establish that a Social Security card is required.

IF YOU HAVE ANY QUESTIONS

If you have any questions about this form or about the evidence documents you must provide, please visit our website at www.socialsecurity.gov for additional information as well as locations of our offices and Social Security Card Centers. You may also call Social Security at 1-800-772-1213. You can also find your nearest office or Card Center in your local phone book.

EVIDENCE DOCUMENTS

The following lists are examples of the types of documents you must provide with your application and are not all inclusive. Call us at 1-800-772-1213 if you cannot provide these documents.

IMPORTANT : If you are completing this application on behalf of someone else, you must provide evidence that shows your authority to sign the application as well as documents to prove your identity and the identity of the person for whom you are filing the application. We can only accept original documents or documents certified by the custodian of the original record. Notarized copies or photocopies which have not been certified by the custodian of the record are not acceptable.

Evidence of Age

In general, you must provide your birth certificate. In some situations, we may accept another document that shows your age. Some of the other documents we may accept are:

- U.S. hospital record of your birth (created at the time of birth)
- Religious record established before age five showing your age or date of birth
- Passport
- Final Adoption Decree (the adoption decree must show that the birth information was taken from the original birth certificate)

Evidence of Identity

You must provide current, unexpired evidence of identity in your legal name. Your legal name will be shown on the Social Security card. Generally, we prefer to see documents issued in the U.S. Documents you submit to establish identity must show your legal name AND provide biographical information (your date of birth, age, or parents' names) **and/or** physical information (photograph, or physical description - height, eye and hair color, etc.). If you send a photo identity document but do not appear in person, the document must show your biographical information (e.g., your date of birth, age, or parents' names). Generally, documents without an expiration date should have been issued within the past two years for adults and within the past four years for children.

As proof of your identity, you must provide a:

- U.S. driver's license; or
- U.S. State-issued non-driver identity card; or
- U.S. passport

If you do not have one of the documents above or cannot get a replacement within 10 work days, we may accept other documents that show your legal name and biographical information, such as a U.S. military identity card, Certificate of Naturalization, employee identity card, certified copy of medical record (clinic, doctor or hospital), health insurance card, Medicaid card, or school identity card/record. For young children, we may accept medical records (clinic, doctor, or hospital) maintained by the medical provider. We may also accept a final adoption decree, or a school identity card, or other school record maintained by the school.

If you are not a U.S. citizen, we must see your current U.S. immigration document(s) and your foreign passport with biographical information or photograph.

WE CANNOT ACCEPT A BIRTH CERTIFICATE, HOSPITAL SOUVENIR BIRTH CERTIFICATE, SOCIAL SECURITY CARD STUB OR A SOCIAL SECURITY RECORD as evidence of identity.

Evidence of U.S. Citizenship

In general, you must provide your U.S. birth certificate or U.S. Passport. Other documents you may provide are a Consular Report of Birth, Certificate of Citizenship, or Certificate of Naturalization.

Evidence of Immigration Status

You must provide a current unexpired document issued to you by the Department of Homeland Security (DHS) showing your immigration status, such as Form I-551, I-94, or I-766. If you are an international student or exchange visitor, you may need to provide additional documents, such as Form I-20, DS-2019, or a letter authorizing employment from your school and employer (F-1) or sponsor (J-1). We CANNOT accept a receipt showing you applied for the document. If you are not authorized to work in the U.S., we can issue you a Social Security card only if you need the number for a valid non-work reason. Your card will be marked to show you cannot work and if you do work, we will notify DHS. See page 3, item 5 for more information.

HOW TO COMPLETE THIS APPLICATION

Complete and sign this application LEGIBLY using ONLY black or blue ink on the attached or downloaded form using only 8 ½" x 11" (or A4 8.25" x 11.7") paper.

GENERAL: Items on the form are self-explanatory or are discussed below. The numbers match the numbered items on the form. If you are completing this form for someone else, please complete the items as they apply to that person.

4. Show the month, day, and full (4 digit) year of birth; for example, "1998" for year of birth.

5. If you check "Legal Alien Not Allowed to Work" or "Other," you must provide a document from a U.S. Federal, State, or local government agency that explains why you need a Social Security number and that you meet all the requirements for the government benefit. NOTE: Most agencies do not require that you have a Social Security number. Contact us to see if your reason qualifies for a Social Security number.

6., 7. Providing race and ethnicity information is voluntary and is requested for informational and statistical purposes only. Your choice whether to answer or not does not affect decisions we make on your application. If you do provide this information, we will treat it very carefully.

9.B., 10.B. If you are applying for an original Social Security card for a child under age 18, you MUST show the parents' Social Security numbers unless the parent was never assigned a Social Security number. If the number is not known and you cannot obtain it, check the "unknown" box.

13. If the date of birth you show in item 4 is different from the date of birth currently shown on your Social Security record, show the date of birth currently shown on your record in item 13 and provide evidence to support the date of birth shown in item 4.

16. Show an address where you can receive your card 7 to 14 days from now.

17. WHO CAN SIGN THE APPLICATION? If you are age 18 or older and are physically and mentally capable of reading and completing the application, you must sign in item 17. If you are under age 18, you may either sign yourself, or a parent or legal guardian may sign for you. If you are over age 18 and cannot sign on your own behalf, a legal guardian, parent, or close relative may generally sign for you. If you cannot sign your name, you should sign with an "X" mark and have two people sign as witnesses in the space beside the mark. Please do not alter your signature by including additional information on the signature line as this may invalidate your application. Call us if you have questions about who may sign your application.

HOW TO SUBMIT THIS APPLICATION

In most cases, you can take or mail this signed application with your documents to any Social Security office. Any documents you mail to us will be returned to you. Go to https://secure.ssa.gov/apps6z/FOLO/fo001.jsp to find the Social Security office or Social Security Card Center that serves your area.

PROTECT YOUR SOCIAL SECURITY NUMBER AND CARD

Protect your SSN card and number from loss and identity theft. DO NOT carry your SSN card with you. Keep it in a secure location and only take it with you when you must show the card; e.g., to obtain a new job, open a new bank account, or to obtain benefits from certain U.S. agencies. Use caution in giving out your Social Security number to others, particularly during phone, mail, email and Internet requests you did not initiate.

PRIVACY ACT STATEMENT
Collection and Use of Personal Information

Sections 205(c) and 702 of the Social Security Act, as amended, allow us to collect this information. Furnishing us this information is voluntary. However, failing to provide all or part of the information may prevent us from assigning you a Social Security number (SSN) and issuing you a new or replacement Social Security card.

We will use the information to assign you an SSN and issue you a new or replacement Social Security card. We may also share your information for the following purposes, called routine uses:

- To Federal, State, and local entities to assist them with administering income maintenance and health maintenance programs, when a Federal statute authorizes them to use the SSN; and,

- To the Department of State for administering the Social Security Act in foreign countries through its facilities and services.

In addition, we may share this information in accordance with the Privacy Act and other Federal laws. For example, where authorized, we may use and disclose this information in computer matching programs, in which our records are compared with other records to establish or verify a person's eligibility for Federal benefit programs and for repayment of incorrect or delinquent debts under these programs.

A list of additional routine uses is available in our Privacy Act System of Records Notice (SORN) 60-0058, entitled Master Files of Social Security Number (SSN) Holders and SSN Applications, as published in the Federal Register (FR) on December 29, 2010, at 75 FR 82121. Additional information, and a full listing of all of our SORNs, is available on our website at www.ssa.gov/privacy.

Paperwork Reduction Act Statement - This information collection meets the requirements of 44 U.S.C. § 3507, as amended by section 2 of the Paperwork Reduction Act of 1995. You do not need to answer these questions unless we display a valid Office of Management and Budget control number. We estimate that it will take about 8.5 to 9.5 minutes to read the instructions, gather the facts, and answer the questions. **SEND OR BRING THE COMPLETED FORM TO YOUR LOCAL SOCIAL SECURITY OFFICE. You can find your local Social Security office through SSA's website at www.socialsecurity.gov. Offices are also listed under U. S. Government agencies in your telephone directory or you may call Social Security at 1-800-772-1213 (TTY 1-800-325-0778).** *You may send comments on our time estimate above to: SSA, 6401 Security Blvd, Baltimore, MD 21235-6401.* ***Send only comments relating to our time estimate to this address, not the completed form.***

Application for a Social Security Card

		First	Full Middle Name	Last
1	**NAME** TO BE SHOWN ON CARD			
	FULL NAME AT BIRTH IF OTHER THAN ABOVE	First	Full Middle Name	Last
	OTHER NAMES USED			

2	Social Security number previously assigned to the person listed in item 1	☐☐☐ ☐☐ ☐☐☐☐

3	**PLACE OF BIRTH** (Do Not Abbreviate) City / State or Foreign Country	Office Use Only FCI	**4**	**DATE OF BIRTH**	MM/DD/YYYY

5	**CITIZENSHIP** (Check One)	☐ U.S. Citizen ☐ Legal Alien Allowed To Work ☐ Legal Alien **Not** Allowed To Work (See Instructions On Page 3) ☐ Other (See Instructions On Page 3)

6	**ETHNICITY** Are You Hispanic or Latino? (Your Response is Voluntary) ☐ Yes ☐ No	**7**	**RACE** Select One or More (Your Response is Voluntary)	☐ Native Hawaiian ☐ American Indian ☐ Other Pacific Islander ☐ Alaska Native ☐ Black/African American ☐ White ☐ Asian

8	**SEX**	☐ Male ☐ Female

		First	Full Middle Name	Last
9	**A. PARENT/ MOTHER'S NAME AT HER BIRTH**			
	B. PARENT/ MOTHER'S SOCIAL SECURITY NUMBER (See instructions for 9B on Page 3)	☐☐☐ ☐☐ ☐☐☐☐ ☐ Unknown		

		First	Full Middle Name	Last
10	**A. PARENT/ FATHER'S NAME**			
	B. PARENT/ FATHER'S SOCIAL SECURITY NUMBER (See instructions for 10B on Page 3)	☐☐☐ ☐☐ ☐☐☐☐ ☐ Unknown		

11	Has the person listed in item 1 or anyone acting on his/her behalf ever filed for or received a Social Security number card before? ☐ Yes (If "yes" answer questions 12-13) ☐ No ☐ Don't Know (If "don't know," skip to question 14.)

		First	Full Middle Name	Last
12	Name shown on the most recent Social Security card issued for the person listed in item 1			

13	Enter any different date of birth if used on an earlier application for a card	MM/DD/YYYY

14	**TODAY'S DATE** MM/DD/YYYY	**15**	**DAYTIME PHONE NUMBER**	Area Code Number

16	**MAILING ADDRESS** (Do Not Abbreviate)	Street Address, Apt. No., PO Box, Rural Route No. City / State/Foreign Country / ZIP Code

I declare under penalty of perjury that I have examined all the information on this form, and on any accompanying statements or forms, and it is true and correct to the best of my knowledge.

17	**YOUR SIGNATURE**	**18**	**YOUR RELATIONSHIP TO THE PERSON IN ITEM 1 IS:** ☐ Self ☐ Natural Or Adoptive Parent ☐ Legal Guardian ☐ Other Specify ________

DO NOT WRITE BELOW THIS LINE (FOR SSA USE ONLY)

NPN			DOC	NTI	CAN		ITV
PBC	EVI	EVA	EVC	PRA	NWR	DNR	UNIT

EVIDENCE SUBMITTED	SIGNATURE AND TITLE OF EMPLOYEE(S) REVIEWING EVIDENCE AND/OR CONDUCTING INTERVIEW
	DATE
	DCL DATE

Appendix: Passport Application Form DS 11

U.S. PASSPORT APPLICATION

PLEASE DETACH AND RETAIN THIS INSTRUCTION SHEET FOR YOUR RECORDS

FOR INFORMATION AND QUESTIONS

Visit the official Department of State website at **travel.state.gov** or contact the National Passport Information Center (NPIC) via toll-free at 1-877-487-2778 (TDD: 1-888-874-7793) and **NPIC@state.gov**. Customer Service Representatives are available Monday-Friday 8:00a.m.-10:00p.m. Eastern Time (excluding federal holidays). Automated information is available 24 hours a day, 7 days a week.

WHAT TO SUBMIT WITH THIS FORM:
1. **PROOF OF U.S. CITIZENSHIP:** Evidence of U.S. citizenship **AND a photocopy** of the front (and back, if there is printed information) must be submitted with your application. The photocopy must be on 8 ½ inch by 11 inch paper, black and white ink, legible, and clear. Evidence that is not damaged, altered, or forged will be returned to you. **Note:** Lawful permanent resident cards submitted with this application will be forwarded to U.S. Citizenship and Immigration Services, if we determine that you are a U.S. citizen.
2. **PROOF OF IDENTITY:** You must present your original identification **AND submit a photocopy** of the front and back with your passport application.
3. **RECENT COLOR PHOTOGRAPH:** Photograph must meet passport requirements – full front view of the face and 2x2 inches in size.
4. **FEES:** Please visit our website at **travel.state.gov** for current fees.

HOW TO SUBMIT THIS FORM:
Complete and submit this application in person to a designated acceptance agent: a clerk of a federal or state court of record or a judge or clerk of a probate court accepting applications; a designated municipal or county official; a designated postal employee at an authorized post office; an agent at a passport agency (by appointment only); or a U.S. consular official at a U.S. Embassy or Consulate, if abroad. To find your nearest acceptance facility, visit **travel.state.gov** or contact the National Passport Information Center at 1-877-487-2778.

Follow the instructions on Page 2 for detailed information to completion and submission of this form.

REQUIREMENTS FOR CHILDREN

- **AS DIRECTED BY PUBLIC LAW 106-113 AND 22 CFR 51.28:**

  To submit an application for a child under age 16 both parents or the child's legal guardian(s) must appear and present the following:
  - Evidence of the child's U.S. citizenship;
  - Evidence of the child's relationship to parents/guardian(s); **AND**
  - Original parental/guardian government-issued identification **AND a photocopy** of the front and back side of presented identification.

  IF ONLY ONE PARENT APPEARS, YOU MUST ALSO SUBMIT ONE OF THE FOLLOWING:
  - Second parent's notarized written statement or DS-3053 (including the child's full name and date of birth) consenting to the passport issuance for the child. The notarized statement <u>cannot</u> be more than **three** months old and <u>must</u> be signed and notarized on the same day, and <u>must</u> come with a photocopy of the front and back side of the second parent's government-issued photo identification; **OR**
  - Second parent's death certificate if second parent is deceased; **OR**
  - Primary evidence of sole authority to apply, such as a court order; **OR**
  - A written statement or DS-5525 (made under penalty of perjury) explaining in detail the second parent's unavailability.

- **AS DIRECTED BY REGULATION 22 C.F.R. 51.21 AND 51.28:**
  - Each minor child applying for a U.S. passport book and/or passport card must appear in person.

PASSPORT VALIDITY LENGTH

If you are 16 years of age or older: Your U.S. passport will be valid for 10 years from the date of issue except where limited by the Secretary of State to a shorter period.

If you are under 16 years of age: Your U.S. passport will be valid for five years from the date of issue except where limited by the Secretary of State to a shorter period.

APPLICANTS WHO HAVE HAD A PREVIOUS U.S. PASSPORT BOOK AND/OR PASSPORT CARD

LOST OR STOLEN - If you cannot submit your valid or potentially valid U.S. passport book and/or passport card with this application and you have not previously submitted Form DS-64, Statement Regarding a Lost or Stolen U.S. Passport, you are required to fill out and submit a DS-64 with this application.

IN MY POSSESSION - If your most recent U.S.passport book and/or passport card was issued less than 15 years ago, and you were over the age of 16 at the time of issuance, you may be eligible to use Form DS-82 to renew your passport by mail.

FAILURE TO PROVIDE INFORMATION REQUESTED ON THIS FORM, INCLUDING YOUR SOCIAL SECURITY NUMBER, MAY RESULT IN SIGNIFICANT PROCESSING DELAYS AND/OR THE DENIAL OF YOUR APPLICATION.

WARNING: False statements made knowingly and willfully in passport applications, including affidavits or other documents submitted to support this application, are punishable by fine and/or imprisonment under U.S. law including the provisions of 18 U.S.C. 1001, 18 U.S.C. 1542, and/or 18 U.S.C. 1621. Alteration or mutilation of a passport issued pursuant to this application is punishable by fine and/or imprisonment under the provisions of 18 U.S.C. 1543. The use of a passport in violation of the restrictions contained herein or of the passport regulations is punishable by fine and/or imprisonment under 18 U.S.C. 1544. All statements and documents are subject to verification.

<h1 style="text-align:center">PROOF OF U.S. CITIZENSHIP</h1>

APPLICANTS BORN IN THE UNITED STATES: Submit a previous U.S. passport or **certified** birth certificate. Passports that are limited in validity will need to be supplemented by other evidence. A birth certificate must include your full name, date and place of birth, sex, date the birth record was filed, the seal or other certification of the official custodian of such records (state, county, or city/town office), and the full names of your parent(s).

- If the birth certificate was filed more than 1 year after the birth: It must be supported by evidence described in the next paragraph.
- If no birth record exists: Submit a registrar's notice to that effect. Also, submit a combination of the evidence listed below, which should include your given name and surname, date and/or place of birth, and the seal or other certification of the office (if customary), and the signature of the issuing official.
  - A hospital birth record;
  - An early baptismal or circumcision certificate;
  - Early census, school, medical, or family Bible records;
  - Insurance files or published birth announcements (such as a newspaper article); and
  - Notarized affidavits (or DS-10, Birth Affidavit) of older blood relatives having knowledge of your birth may be submitted **in addition** to some of the records listed above.

APPLICANTS BORN OUTSIDE THE UNITED STATES: Submit a previous U.S. passport, Certificate of Naturalization, Certificate of Citizenship, Consular Report of Birth Abroad, or evidence described below:

- If you claim citizenship through naturalization of parent(s): Submit the Certificate(s) of Naturalization of your parent(s), your foreign birth certificate (and official translation if the document is not in English), proof of your admission to the United States for permanent residence, **and** your parents' marriage/certificate and/or evidence that you were in the legal and physical custody of your U.S. citizen parent, if applicable.
- If you claim citizenship through birth abroad to at least one U.S. citizen parent: Submit a Consular Report of Birth (Form FS-240), Certification of Birth (Form DS-1350 or FS-545), or your foreign birth certificate (and official translation if the document is not in English), proof of U.S. citizenship of your parent, your parents' marriage certificate, **and** an affidavit showing all of your U.S. citizen parents' periods and places of residence/physical presence in the United States and abroad before your birth.
- If you claim citizenship through adoption by a U.S. citizen parent(s): Submit evidence of your permanent residence status, full and final adoption, **and** your U.S. citizen parent(s) evidence of legal and physical custody. (**NOTE**: Acquisition of U.S. citizenship for persons born abroad and adopted only applies if the applicant was born on or after 02/28/1983.)

ADDITIONAL EVIDENCE: You must establish your citizenship to the satisfaction of the acceptance agent and Passport Services. We may ask you to provide additional evidence to establish your claim to U.S. citizenship. Visit travel.state.gov for details.

<h2 style="text-align:center">PROOF OF IDENTITY</h2>

You may submit items such as the following containing your signature AND a photograph that is a good likeness of you: previous or current U.S. passport book; previous or current U.S. passport card; driver's license (not temporary or learner's license); Certificate of Naturalization; Certificate of Citizenship; military identification; or federal, state, or municipal government employee identification card. Temporary or altered documents are not acceptable.

You must establish your identity to the satisfaction of the acceptance agent and Passport Services. We may ask you to provide additional evidence to establish your identity. If you have changed your name, please see **travel.state.gov** for instructions.

IF YOU CANNOT PROVIDE DOCUMENTARY EVIDENCE OF IDENTITY as stated above, you must appear with an IDENTIFYING WITNESS, who is a U.S. citizen, non-citizen U.S. national, or permanent resident alien that has known you for at least two years. Your witness must prove his or her identity and complete and sign an Affidavit of Identifying Witness (Form DS-71) before the acceptance agent. You must also submit some identification of your own.

<h2 style="text-align:center">COLOR PHOTOGRAPH</h2>

Submit a color photograph of you alone, sufficiently recent to be a good likeness of you (taken within the last six months), and 2x2 inches in size. The image size measured from the bottom of your chin to the top of your head (including hair) should not be less than 1 inch, and not more than 1 3/8 inches. The photograph must be in color, clear, with a full front view of your face. The photograph must be taken with a neutral facial expression (preferred) or a natural smile, and with both eyes open and be printed on photo quality paper with a plain light (white or off-white) background. The photograph must be taken in normal street attire, without a hat, or head covering unless a signed statement is submitted by the applicant verifying that the hat or head covering is part of recognized, traditional religious attire that is customarily or required to be worn continuously when in public or a signed doctor's statement is submitted verifying the item is used daily for medical purposes. Headphones, "bluetooth", or similar devices must not be worn in the passport photograph. Glasses or other eyewear are not acceptable unless you provide a signed statement from a doctor explaining why you cannot remove them due to medical reasons (e.g., during the recovery period from eye surgery). Any photograph retouched so that your appearance is changed is unacceptable. A snapshot, most vending machine prints, hand-held self portraits, and magazine or full-length photographs are unacceptable. A digital photo must meet the previously stated qualifications, and will be accepted for use at the discretion of Passport Services. Visit our website at **travel.state.gov** for details and information.

<h2 style="text-align:center">FEES</h2>

*FEES ARE LISTED ON OUR WEBSITE AT **TRAVEL.STATE.GOV**. BY LAW, THE PASSPORT FEES ARE NON-REFUNDABLE.*

- **The passport application fee, security surcharge, and expedite fee may be paid in any of the following forms:** Checks (personal, certified, or traveler's) with the applicant's full name and date of birth printed on the front; major credit card (Visa, Master Card, American Express, and Discover); bank draft or cashier's check; money order (U.S. Postal, international, currency exchange), or if abroad, the foreign currency equivalent, or a check drawn on a U.S. bank. All fees should be payable to the "U.S. Department of State" or if abroad, the appropriate U.S. Embassy or U.S. Consulate. When applying at a designated acceptance facility, the execution fee will be paid separately and should be made payable to the acceptance facility. **NOTE: Some designated acceptance facilities do not accept credit cards as a form of payment.**

- **For faster processing**, you may request expedited service. Please include the expedite fee in your payment. Our website contains updated information regarding fees and processing times for expedited service. Expedited service is only available for passports mailed in the United States and Canada.

- **OVERNIGHT DELIVERY SERVICE** is only available for passport book mailings in the United States. Please include the appropriate fee with your payment.

- An additional fee will be charged when, upon your request, the U.S. Department of State verifies issuance of a previous U.S. passport or Consular Report of Birth Abroad because you are unable to submit evidence of U.S. citizenship.

- **For applicants with U.S. government or military authorization for no-fee passports**, no fees are charged except the execution fee when applying at a designated acceptance facility.

NOTE REGARDING MAILING OF YOUR PASSPORT(S)

Passport Services will not mail a U.S. passport to a private address outside the United States or Canada. If you do not live at the address listed in the "mailing address", then you must put the name of the person and mark it as "In Care Of" in item # 8. If your mailing address changes prior to receipt of your new passport, please contact the National Passport Information Center.

If you choose to provide your email address in Item #6 on this application, Passport Services may use that information to contact you in the event there is a problem with your application or if you need to provide information to us.

You may receive your newly issued passport book and/or card and your returned citizenship evidence in **two separate mailings**. If you are applying for both a U.S. passport book and passport card, **you may receive three separate mailings**; one with your returned citizenship evidence, one with your newly issued passport book, and one with your newly issued passport card.

FEDERAL TAX LAW

Section 6039E of the Internal Revenue Code (26 U.S.C. 6039E) and 22 U.S.C 2714a(f) require you to provide your Social Security number (SSN), if you have one, when you apply for or renew a U.S. passport. If you have never been issued a SSN, you must enter zeros in box #5 of this form. If you are residing abroad, you must also provide the name of the foreign country in which you are residing. The U.S. Department of State must provide your SSN and foreign residence information to the U.S. Department of the Treasury. If you fail to provide the information, your application may be denied and you are subject to a $500 penalty enforced by the IRS. All questions on this matter should be referred to the nearest IRS office.

NOTICE TO CUSTOMERS APPLYING OUTSIDE A DEPARTMENT OF STATE FACILITY

If you send us a check, it will be converted into an electronic funds transfer (EFT). This means we will copy your check and use the account information on it to electronically debit your account for the amount of the check. The debit from your account will usually occur within 24 hours and will be shown on your regular account statement.

You will not receive your original check back. We will destroy your original check, but we will keep the copy of it. If the EFT cannot be processed for technical reasons, you authorize us to process the copy in place of your original check. If the EFT cannot be completed because of insufficient funds, we may try to make the transfer up to two times, and we will charge you a one-time fee of $25, which we will also collect by EFT.

FEE REMITTANCE

Passport service fees are established by law and regulation (see 22 U.S.C. 214, 22 C.F.R. 22.1, and 22 C.F.R. 51.50-56), and are collected at the time you apply for the passport service. If the Department fails to receive full payment of the applicable fees because, for example, your check is returned for any reason or you dispute a passport fee charge to your credit card, the U.S. Department of State will take action to collect the delinquent fees from you under 22 C.F.R. Part 34, and the Federal Claims Collection Standards (see 31 C.F.R. Parts 900-904). In accordance with the Debt Collection Improvement Act (Pub.L. 104-134), if the fees remain unpaid after 180 days and no repayment arrangements have been made, the Department will refer the debt to the U.S. Department of Treasury for collection. Debt collection procedures used by U.S. Department of Treasury may include referral of the debt to private collection agencies, reporting of the debt to credit bureaus, garnishment of private wages and administrative offset of the debt by reducing, or withholding eligible federal payments (e.g., tax refunds, social security payments, federal retirement, etc.) by the amount of your debt, including any interest penalties or other costs incurred. In addition, non-payment of passport fees may result in the invalidation of your passport. An invalidated passport cannot be used for travel.

USE OF SOCIAL SECURITY NUMBER

Your Social Security number will be provided to U.S. Department of Treasury, used in connection with debt collection and checked against lists of persons ineligible or potentially ineligible to receive a U.S. passport, among other authorized uses.

NOTICE TO APPLICANTS FOR OFFICIAL, DIPLOMATIC, OR NO-FEE PASSPORTS

You may use this application if you meet all of the provisions listed on Instruction Page 2; however, you must CONSULT YOUR SPONSORING AGENCY FOR INSTRUCTIONS ON PROPER ROUTING PROCEDURES BEFORE FORWARDING THIS APPLICATION. Your completed passport will be released to your sponsoring agency for forwarding to you.

PROTECT YOURSELF AGAINST IDENTITY THEFT!
REPORT YOUR LOST OR STOLEN PASSPORT BOOK OR PASSPORT CARD!

For more information regarding reporting a lost or stolen U.S. passport book or passport card (Form DS-64), or to determine your eligibility for a passport renewal (Form DS-82), call NPIC at 1-877-487-2778 or visit **travel.state.gov**.

NOTICE TO U.S. PASSPORT CARD APPLICANTS

The maximum number of letters provided for your given name (first and middle) on the U.S. passport card is 24 characters. The 24 characters may be shortened due to printing restrictions. If both your given names are more than 24 characters, you must shorten one of your given names you list on item 1 of this form.

U.S. passports, either in book or card format, are only issued to U.S. citizens or non-citizen U.S. nationals. Each person must obtain his or her own U.S. passport book or U.S. passport card. The passport card is a U.S. passport issued in card format. Like the traditional U.S. passport book, it reflects the bearer's origin, identity, and nationality, and is subject to existing passport laws and regulations. **Unlike the U.S. passport book, the U.S. passport card is valid only for entry at land border crossings and sea ports of entry when traveling from Canada, Mexico, the Caribbean, and Bermuda.** The U.S. passport card is **not** valid for international air travel.

APPLICATION FOR A U.S. PASSPORT
Please Print Legibly Using Black Ink Only

OMB CONTROL NO.: 1405-0004
EXPIRATION DATE: 4-30-2021
ESTIMATED BURDEN: 85 MIN

Attention: Read WARNING on page 1 of instructions
Please select the document(s) for which you are applying:

☐ U.S. Passport Book   ☐ U.S. Passport Card   ☐ Both

The U.S. passport card is **not** valid for international air travel. For more information see page 1 of instructions.

☐ Regular Book (Standard)   ☐ Large Book (Non-Standard)

Note: The large book option is for those who frequently travel abroad during the passport validity period, and is recommended for applicants who have previously required the addition of visa pages.

☐ D ☐ O ☐ Dep DOTS ______
End. # ______   Exp. ______

1. Name Last

First   Middle

2. Date of Birth *(mm/dd/yyyy)*

3. Sex M F

4. Place of Birth *(City & State if in the U.S., or City & Country as it is presently known.)*

5. Social Security Number

6. Email *(Info alerts offered at travel.state.gov)* @

7. Primary Contact Phone Number

8. Mailing Address: Line 1: Street/RFD#, P.O. Box, or URB.

Address Line 2: **Clearly label** Apartment, Company, Suite, Unit, Building, Floor, In Care Of or Attention if applicable. *(e.g., In Care Of - Jane Doe, Apt # 100)*

City   State   Zip Code   Country, if outside the United States

9. List all other names you have used. *(Examples: Birth Name, Maiden, Previous Marriage, Legal Name Change. Attach additional pages if needed)*

A.   B.

→ STOP! CONTINUE TO PAGE 2 →
DO NOT SIGN APPLICATION UNTIL REQUESTED TO DO SO BY AUTHORIZED AGENT

STAPLE STAPLE

FROM 1" TO 1 3/8"

2" X 2"   2" X 2"

STAPLE STAPLE

Attach a color photograph taken within the last six months

☐ Acceptance Agent   ☐ (Vice) Consul USA

☐ Passport Staff Agent

(Seal)

Identifying Documents - Applicant or Mother/Father/Parent on Second Signature Line (if identifying minor)

☐ Driver's License ☐ State Issued ID Card ☐ Passport ☐ Military ☐ Other ______

Name ______

Issue Date *(mm/dd/yyyy)*   Exp. Date *(mm/dd/yyyy)*   State of Issuance

ID No   Country of Issuance

Identifying Documents - Applicant or Mother/Father/Parent on Third Signature Line (if identifying minor)

☐ Driver's License ☐ State Issued ID Card ☐ Passport ☐ Military ☐ Other ______

Name ______

Issue Date *(mm/dd/yyyy)*   Exp. Date *(mm/dd/yyyy)*   State of Issuance

ID No   Country of Issuance

I declare under penalty of perjury all of the following: 1) I am a citizen or non-citizen national of the United States and have not, since acquiring U.S. citizenship or nationality, performed any of the acts listed under "Acts or Conditions" on page four of the instructions of this application (unless explanatory statement is attached); 2) the statements made on the application are true and correct; 3) I have not knowingly and willfully made false statements or included false documents in support of this application; 4) the photograph attached to this application is a genuine, current photograph of me; and 5) I have read and understood the warning on page one of the instructions to the application form.

Name of courier company *(if applicable)*

Facility Name/Location

Facility ID Number

Agent ID Number

X ______
Applicant's Legal Signature - age 16 and older

X ______
Mother/Father/Parent/Legal Guardian's Signature (if identifying minor)

X ______
Mother/Father/Parent/Legal Guardian's Signature (if identifying minor)

Signature of person authorized to accept applications   Date

For Issuing Office Only ——→ Bk ______ Card ______ EF ______ Postage ______ Execution ______ Other ______

* DS 11 C 09 2013 1 *

DS-11   06-2016   Page 1 of 2

Name of Applicant (*Last, First, & Middle*)	**Date of Birth** (*mm/dd/yyyy*)

10. Parental Information
Mother/Father/Parent - First & Middle Name   Last Name (*at Parent's Birth*)

Date of Birth (*mm/dd/yyyy*)   Place of Birth   Sex   U.S. Citizen?
                                                                   Male   Yes
                                                                    Female   No

Mother/Father/Parent - First & Middle Name   Last Name (*at Parent's Birth*)

Date of Birth (*mm/dd/yyyy*)   Place of Birth   Sex   U.S. Citizen?
                                                                    Male   Yes
                                                                    Female   No

11. Have you ever been married?   Yes   No   *If yes, complete the remaining items in #11.*
Full Name of Current Spouse or Most Recent Spouse   Date of Birth (mm/dd/yyyy)   Place of Birth

U.S. Citizen?   Date of Marriage   Have you ever been widowed or divorced?   Widow/Divorce Date
  Yes   No   (*mm/dd/yyyy*)   Yes   No   (*mm/dd/yyyy*)

12. Additional Contact Phone Number   **13. Occupation** (*if age 16 or older*)   **14. Employer or School** (*if applicable*)
                                    Home   Cell
                                    Work

15. Height   **16. Hair Color**   **17. Eye Color**   **18. Travel Plans**
                                     Departure Date (*mm/dd/yyyy*)   Return Date (*mm/dd/yyyy*)   Countries to be Visited

19. Permanent Address - *If P.O. Box is listed under Mailing Address* **or** *if residence is different from Mailing Address.*
Street/RFD # or URB (**No P.O. Box**)   Apartment/Unit

City   State   Zip Code

20. Emergency Contact - *Provide the information of a person not traveling with you to be contacted in the event of an emergency.*
Name   Address: Street/RFD # or P.O. Box   Apartment/Unit

City   State   Zip Code   Phone Number   Relationship

21. Have you ever applied for or been issued a U.S. Passport Book or Passport Card?   Yes   No   *If yes, complete the remaining items in #21.*
Name as printed on your most recent passport book   Most recent passport book number   Most recent passport book issue date (*mm/dd/yyyy*)

Status of your most recent passport book: Submitting with application   Stolen   Lost   In my possession (*if expired*)

Name as printed on your most recent passport card   Most recent passport card number   Most recent passport card issue date (*mm/dd/yyyy*)

Status of your most recent passport card: Submitting with application   Stolen   Lost   In my possession (*if expired*)

PLEASE DO NOT WRITE BELOW THIS LINE - FOR ISSUING OFFICE ONLY

Name as it appears on citizenship evidence

☐ Birth Certificate   SR   CR   City   Filed: Issued:

☐ Nat. / Citz. Cert.   USCIS   USDC   Date/Place Acquired: A#

☐ Report of Birth   Filed/Place:

☐ Passport   C/R   S/R   Per PIERS   #/DOI:

☐ Other:

☐ Attached:

☐ P/C of Citz ☐ P/C of ID ☐ DS-71 ☐ DS-3053 ☐ DS-64 ☐ DS-5520 ☐ DS-5525 ☐ PAW ☐ NPIC ☐ IRL ☐ Citz W/S   * DS 11 C 09 2013 2 *

Appendix: Passport Application Form DS 82

U.S. PASSPORT RENEWAL APPLICATION FOR ELIGIBLE INDIVIDUALS
PLEASE DETACH AND RETAIN THIS INSTRUCTION SHEET FOR YOUR RECORDS

Mailing Date of Application: _______________________________

CAN I USE THIS FORM?
Complete the checklist to determine your eligibility to use this form

I can submit my most recent U.S. passport book and/or U.S. passport card with this application.	☐ Yes ☐ No
I was at least 16 years old when my most recent U.S. passport book and/or passport card was issued.	☐ Yes ☐ No
I was issued my most recent U.S. passport book and/or passport card less than 15 years ago.	☐ Yes ☐ No
The U.S. passport book and/or U.S. passport card that I am renewing has not been mutilated, damaged, lost, stolen or subsequently found.	☐ Yes ☐ No
My U.S. passport has not been limited from the normal ten year validity period due to passport damage/mutilation, multiple passport thefts/losses, or non-compliance with 22 C.F.R. 51.41. (Please refer to the back pages of your U.S. passport book for endorsement information).	☐ Yes ☐ No
I use the same name as on my most recent U.S. passport book and/or U.S. passport card. --OR-- I have had my name changed by marriage or court order and can submit proper certified documentation to reflect my name change.	☐ Yes ☐ No

If you answered NO to any of the statements above,
STOP - You cannot use this form!

You must apply on application form DS-11 by making a personal appearance before an acceptance agent authorized to accept passport applications. Visit **travel.state.gov** to find your nearest acceptance facility.

U.S. passports, either in book or card format, are only issued to U.S. Citizens or non-citizen U.S. nationals. Each person must obtain his or her own U.S. passport book or passport card. The passport card is a U.S. passport issued in card format. Like the traditional U.S. passport book, it reflects the bearer's origin, identity, and nationality, and is subject to existing passport laws and regulations. Unlike the U.S. passport book, the U.S. passport card is valid only for entry at land border crossings and sea ports of entry when traveling from Canada, Mexico, the Caribbean, and Bermuda. The U.S. passport card is not valid for international air travel.

PLEASE NOTE: Your new passport will have a different passport number than your previous passport.

FOR INFORMATION AND QUESTIONS

Visit the Department of State website at **travel.state.gov** or contact the National Passport Information Center (NPIC) toll-free at 1-877-487-2778 (TDD: 1-888-874-7793) or by email at **NPIC@state.gov**. Customer Service Representatives are available Monday-Friday 8:00a.m.-10:00p.m. and Saturday 10:00a.m.-3:00p.m. Eastern Time (excluding federal holidays). Automated information is available 24 hours a day, 7 days a week.

FAILURE TO PROVIDE INFORMATION REQUESTED ON THIS FORM, INCLUDING YOUR SOCIAL SECURITY NUMBER, MAY RESULT IN SIGNIFICANT PROCESSING DELAYS AND/OR THE DENIAL OF YOUR APPLICATION

NOTICE TO APPLICANTS RESIDING ABROAD

United States citizens residing outside the U.S. or Canada **CANNOT** submit this form to domestic addresses listed on the Instruction Page 2. Such applicants should visit www.usembassy.gov to find the nearest U.S. Embassy or Consulate for procedures for applying outside the United States.

WARNING: False statements made knowingly and willfully in passport applications, including affidavits or other documents submitted to support this application, are punishable by fine and/or imprisonment under U.S. law, including the provisions of 18 U.S.C. 1001, 18 U.S.C. 1542, and/or 18 U.S.C. 1621. Alteration or mutilation of a passport issued pursuant to this application is punishable by fine and/or imprisonment under the provisions of 18 U.S.C. 1543. The use of a passport in violation of the restrictions contained therein or of the passport regulations is punishable by fine and/or imprisonment under 18 U.S.C. 1544. All statements and documents are subject to verification.

See page 2 of the instructions for detailed information on the completion and submission of this form.

WHAT DO I SEND WITH THIS APPLICATION FORM?

- **Your most recent U.S. passport book and/or card;**
- **A certified copy of your marriage certificate or court order if your name has changed;**
- **Fees; and**
- **A recent, color photograph.**

See below for more detailed information

1. YOUR MOST RECENTLY ISSUED U.S. PASSPORT (BOOK AND/OR CARD FORMAT).

- Submit your **most recently issued** U.S. passport book and/or card. When submitting a U.S. passport book and/or card with this form, please verify that the document was issued at age 16 or older in your current name (or see item #2 below) and issued within the past 15 years. You are also eligible to use this form if you currently have a U.S. passport book and/or card that complies with the previously listed criteria, and would like to obtain a alternative product (U.S. passport book and/or card) for the first time. However, you must submit the product you currently have (U.S. passport book and/or card) with this application. If your U.S. passport book and/or card has been lost, stolen, damaged, or mutilated, you must apply on the DS-11 application form as specified below.

2. A CERTIFIED MARRIAGE CERTIFICATE OR COURT ORDER (PHOTOCOPIES ARE NOT ACCEPTED).

- If the name you are currently using differs from the name on your most recent U.S. passport, you must submit a certified copy of your marriage certificate or court order showing the change of name. All documents will be returned to you by mail. If you are unable to document your name change in this manner, you must apply on the DS-11 application form by making a personal appearance at (1) a passport agency; (2) U.S. embassy or consulate, if abroad; (3) any federal or state court of record or any probate court accepting passport applications; (4) a designated municipal or county official; or (5) a post office, which has been selected to accept passport applications.

3. THE CURRENT PASSPORT FEE (DO NOT SEND ACCEPTANCE AGENT FEE WITH THIS FORM).

- Enclose the fee in the form of a personal check or money order. **MAKE CHECKS PAYABLE TO "U.S. DEPARTMENT OF STATE." THE FULL NAME AND DATE OF BIRTH OF THE APPLICANT MUST BE TYPED OR PRINTED ON THE FRONT OF THE CHECK. <u>DO NOT SEND CASH</u>** Passport Services cannot be responsible for cash sent through the mail. By law, the fees are non-refundable. Please visit our website at **travel.state.gov** for detailed information regarding current fees. Newly issued passport cards are delivered via first class mail only.

<u>OVERNIGHT DELIVERY SERVICE</u> is only available for passport book (and not passport card) mailings in the United States. Please include the appropriate fee with your application.

<u>FOR FASTER PROCESSING</u>, you may request expedited service. Please include the expedited fee with your application. **Please write "Expedite" on the outer envelope when mailing. Also, <u>TO ENSURE MINIMAL PROCESSING TIME</u> for expedited applications, Passport Services recommends using overnight delivery when submitting the application AND including the appropriate postage fee for return overnight delivery for the newly issued passport book.** Expedited service is only available for passports mailed in the United States and Canada. Please visit **travel.state.gov** for updated information regarding fees, processing times, or to check the status of your passport application online.

4. A RECENT, COLOR PHOTOGRAPH.

- Submit a color photograph of you alone, sufficiently recent to be a good likeness of you **(taken within the last six months)**, and 2x2 inches in size. The image size measured from the bottom of your chin to the top of your head (including hair) should not be less than 1 inch, and not more than 1 3/8 inches. The photograph must be in color, clear, with a full front view of your face. The photograph must be taken with a neutral facial expression (preferred) or a natural smile, and with both eyes open and be printed on photo quality paper with a plain light (white or off-white) background. The photograph must be taken in normal street attire, without a hat, or head covering unless a signed statement is submitted by the applicant verifying that the hat or head covering is part of recognized, traditional religious attire that is customarily or required to be worn continuously when in public or a signed doctor's statement is submitted verifying the item is used daily for medical purposes. Headphones, "bluetooth", or similar devices must not be worn in the passport photograph. Glasses or other eyewear are not acceptable unless you provide a signed statement from a doctor explaining why you cannot remove them due to medical reasons (e.g., during the recovery period from eye surgery). Any photograph retouched so that your appearance is changed is unacceptable. A snapshot, most vending machine prints, hand-held self portraits, and magazine or full-length photographs are unacceptable. A digital photo must meet the previously stated qualifications, and will be accepted for use at the discretion of Passport Services. Visit our website at **travel.state.gov** for details and information.

<u>USE CAUTION WHEN STAPLING YOUR PHOTO</u>: Use 4 staples vertically in the corners as close to the outer edge as possible. Do not bend photo.

WHERE DO I MAIL THIS APPLICATION?

FOR ROUTINE SERVICE (If you live in CA, FL, IL, MN, NY, or TX):
National Passport Processing Center
P.O. Box 640155
Irving, TX 75064-0155

FOR ROUTINE SERVICE (If you live in any other state or Canada):
National Passport Processing Center
P.O. Box 90955
Philadelphia, PA 19190-0155

FOR EXPEDITED SERVICE (Additional Fee, any state or Canada):
National Passport Processing Center
P.O. Box 90955
Philadelphia, PA 19190-0955

<u>Because of the sensitivity of the enclosed documents, Passport Services recommends using trackable mailing service when submitting your application.</u>

NOTE REGARDING MAILING ADDRESSES: Passport Services does not send mail to a private address outside the United States or Canada. If you do not live at the address listed in the "Mailing Address", then you must put the name of the person and mark it as "In Care Of." If your mailing address changes prior to receipt of your new passport, please contact the National Passport Information Center (NPIC) at 1-877-487-2778 or visit **travel.state.gov**.

You may receive your newly issued document and your returned citizenship evidence in separate mailings. If you are applying for both a passport book and/or card, you may receive **three separate mailings**: one with your returned citizenship evidence; one with your newly issued passport book, and one with your newly printed passport card.

If you choose to provide your email address in Item #6 on this application, Passport Services may use that address to contact you in the event there is a problem with your application or if you need to provide additional information to us.

FEDERAL TAX LAW

Section 6039E of the Internal Revenue Code (26 USC 6039E) and 22 U.S.C. 2714a(f) require you to provide your Social Security number (SSN), if you have one, when you apply for or renew a U.S. passport. If you have never been issued a SSN, enter zeros in box #5 of this form. If you are residing abroad, you must also provide the name of the foreign country in which you are residing. The U.S. Department of State must provide your SSN and foreign residence information to the U.S. Department of Treasury. If you fail to provide the information, you are subject to a $500 penalty enforced by the IRS. All questions on this matter should be directed to the nearest IRS office.

NOTICE TO CUSTOMERS APPLYING OUTSIDE A DEPARTMENT OF STATE FACILITY

If you send us a check, it will be converted into an electronic funds transfer (EFT). This means we will copy your check and use the account information on it to electronically debit your account for the amount of the check. The debit from your account will usually occur within 24 hours and will be shown on your regular account statement.

You will not receive your original check back. We will destroy your original check, but we will keep the copy of it. If the EFT cannot be processed for technical reasons, you authorize us to process the copy in place of your original check. If the EFT cannot be completed because of insufficient funds, we may try to make the transfer up to two times, and we will charge you a one-time fee of $25, which we will also collect by EFT.

FEE REMITTANCE

Passport service fees are established by law and regulation (see 22 U.S.C. 214, 22 C.F.R. 22.1, and 22 C.F.R. 51.50-56), and are collected at the time you apply for the passport service. If the Department fails to receive full payment of the applicable fees because, for example, your check is returned for any reason or you dispute a passport fee charge to your credit card, the U.S. Department of State will take action to collect the delinquent fees from you under 22 C.F.R. Part 34, and the Federal Claims Collection Standards (see 31 C.F.R. Parts 900-904). In accordance with the Debt Collection Improvement Act (Pub.L. 104-134), if the fees remain unpaid after 180 days and no repayment arrangements have been made, the Department will refer the debt to the U.S. Department of Treasury for collection. Debt collection procedures used by the U.S. Department of Treasury may include referral of the debt to private collection agencies, reporting of the debt to credit bureaus, garnishment of private wages and administrative offset of the debt by reducing, or withholding eligible federal payments (e.g., tax refunds, social security payments, federal retirement, etc.) by the amount of your debt, including any interest penalties or other costs incurred. In addition, non-payment of passport fees may result in the invalidation of your U.S. passport book and/or card. An invalidated passport book or card cannot be used for travel.

USE OF SOCIAL SECURITY NUMBER

Your Social Security number will be provided to the U.S. Department of Treasury, used in connection with debt collection and checked against lists of persons ineligible or potentially ineligible to receive a U.S. passport book and/or card, among other authorized uses.

NOTICE TO APPLICANTS FOR OFFICIAL, DIPLOMATIC, OR NO-FEE PASSPORTS

You may use this application if you meet all of the provisions listed on Instruction Page 2; however, you must CONSULT YOUR SPONSORING AGENCY FOR INSTRUCTIONS ON PROPER ROUTING PROCEDURES BEFORE FORWARDING THIS APPLICATION. Your completed passport will be released to your sponsoring agency for forwarding to you.

IMPORTANT NOTICE TO APPLICANTS WHO HAVE LOST OR HAD A PREVIOUS U.S. PASSPORT BOOK AND/OR PASSPORT CARD STOLEN

A United States citizen may not normally bear more than one valid or potentially valid U.S. passport book or more than one valid or potentially valid U.S. passport card at a time. Therefore, when a valid or potentially valid U.S. passport book or U.S passport card cannot be presented with a new application, it is necessary to submit a Form DS-64, Statement Regarding a Lost or Stolen U.S. Passport. Your statement must detail why the previous U.S. passport book or U.S. passport card cannot be presented.

The information you provide regarding your lost or stolen U.S. passport book or passport card will be placed into our Consular Lost or Stolen Passport System. This system is designed to prevent the misuse of your lost or stolen U.S. passport book or passport card. Anyone using the passport book or passport card reported as lost or stolen may be detained upon entry into the United States. Should you locate the U.S. passport book or passport card reported lost or stolen at a later time, report it as found, and submit it for cancellation. <u>It has been invalidated</u> You may not use that passport book or passport card for travel.

PROTECT YOURSELF AGAINST IDENTITY THEFT!
REPORT YOUR LOST OR STOLEN U.S. PASSPORT BOOK OR PASSPORT CARD!

For more information or to report your lost or stolen U.S. passport book or passport card by phone, call NPIC at:
1-877-487-2778 or visit our website at **travel.state.gov**

NOTICE TO U.S. PASSPORT <u>CARD</u> APPLICANTS ONLY

The maximum number of letters provided for your given name (first and middle) on the U.S. passport card is 24 characters. The 24 characters may be shortened due to printing restrictions. If both your given names are more than 24 characters, you must shorten one of your given names on item 1 of this form.

ACTS OR CONDITIONS

(If any of the below-mentioned acts or conditions have been performed by or apply to the applicant, the portion which applies should be lined out, and a supplementary explanatory statement under oath (or affirmation) by the applicant should be attached and made a part of this application.)

I have not, since acquiring United States citizenship/nationality, been naturalized as a citizen of a foreign state; taken an oath or made an affirmation or other formal declaration of allegiance to a foreign state; entered or served in the armed forces of a foreign state; accepted or performed the duties of any office, post, or employment under the government of a foreign state or political subdivision thereof; made a formal renunciation of nationality either in the United States, or before a diplomatic or consular officer of the United States in a foreign state; or been convicted by a court or court martial of competent jurisdiction of committing any act of treason against, or attempting by force to overthrow, or bearing arms against the United States, or conspiring to overthrow, put down, or to destroy by force, the government of the United States.

Furthermore, I have not been convicted of a federal or state drug offense or convicted of a "sex tourism" crime, and I am not the subject of an outstanding federal, state, or local warrant of arrest for a felony; a criminal court order forbidding my departure from the United States; or a subpoena received from the United States in a matter involving federal prosecution for, or grand jury investigation of, a felony.

PRIVACY ACT STATEMENT

AUTHORITIES: Collection of this information is authorized by 22 U.S.C. 211a et seq.; 8 U.S.C. 1104; 26 U.S.C. 6039E, 22 U.S.C. 2714a(f), Section 236 of the Admiral James W. Nance and Meg Donovan Foreign Relations Authorization Act, Fiscal Years 2000 and 2001; Executive Order 11295 (August 5, 1966); and 22 C.F.R. parts 50 and 51.

PURPOSE: We are requesting this information in order to determine your eligibility to be issued a U.S. passport. Your Social Security number is used to verify your identity.

ROUTINE USES: Your Social Security number will be provided to the Department of the Treasury and may be used in connection with debt collection, among other purposes authorized and generally described in this section. This information may be disclosed to another domestic government agency, a private contractor, a foreign government agency, or to a private person or private employer in accordance with certain approved routine uses. These routine uses include, but are not limited to, law enforcement activities, employment verification, fraud prevention, border security, counterterrorism, litigation activities, and activities that meet the Secretary of State's responsibility to protect U.S. citizens and non-citizen nationals abroad. More information on the Routine Uses for the system can be found in System of Records Notices State-05, Overseas Citizen Services Records and State-26, Passport Records.

DISCLOSURE: Providing information on this form is voluntary. Be advised, however, that failure to provide the information requested on this form may cause delays in processing your U.S. passport application and/or could also result in the refusal or denial of your application.

Failure to provide your Social Security number may result in the denial of your application (consistent with 22 U.S.C. 2714a(f)) and may subject you to penalty enforced by the Internal Revenue Service, as described in the Federal Tax Law section of the instructions to this form.

ELECTRONIC PASSPORT STATEMENT

The U.S. Department of State now issues a type of passport book containing an embedded electronic chip called an "Electronic Passport". The electronic passport book continues to be proof of the bearer's United States citizenship/nationality and identity, and looks and functions in the same way as a passport without a chip. The addition of an electronic chip in the back cover enables the passport book to carry a duplicate electronic copy of all information from the data page. The electronic passport book is usable at all ports-of-entry, including those that do not yet have electronic chip readers.

Use of the electronic format provides the traveler the additional security protections inherent in chip technology. Moreover, when used at ports-of-entry equipped with electronic chip readers, the electronic passport book provides for faster clearance through some of the port-of-entry processes.

The electronic passport book does not require special handling or treatment, but like previous versions should be protected from extreme heat, bending, and from immersion in water. The electronic chip must be read using specially formatted readers, which protects the data on the chip from unauthorized reading.

The cover of the electronic passport book is printed with a special symbol representing the embedded chip. The symbol  will appear in port-of-entry areas where the electronic passport book can be read.

PAPERWORK REDUCTION ACT STATEMENT

Public reporting burden for this collection of information is estimated to average 40 minutes per response, including the time required for searching existing data sources, gathering the necessary data, providing the information and/or documentation required, and reviewing the final collection. You do not have to supply this information unless this collection displays a currently valid OMB control number. If you have comments on the accuracy of this burden estimate and/or recommendations for reducing it, please send them to: Passport Forms Officer, U.S. Department of State, CA/PPT/S/L, 44132 Mercure Cir, P.O. Box 1227 Sterling, Virginia 20166-1227.

 **U.S. PASSPORT RENEWAL APPLICATION FOR ELIGIBLE INDIVIDUALS**

Please Print Legibly Using Black Ink Only

OMB CONTROL NO. 1405-0020
OMB EXPIRATION DATE: 10-31-2020
ESTIMATED BURDEN: 40 MIN

Attention: Read WARNING on page 1 of instructions
Please select the document(s) for which you are applying:

☐ U.S. Passport Book   ☐ U.S. Passport Card   ☐ Both

The U.S. passport card is **not** valid for international air travel. For more information see page 1 of instructions.

☐ Regular Book (Standard)   ☐ Large Book (Non-Standard)

Note: The large book option is for those who frequently travel abroad during the passport validity period, and is recommended for applicants who have previously required the addition of visa pages.

1. Name Last

First   Middle

☐ D   ☐ O   ☐ DP DOTS Code _______

End. # _______   Exp. _______

2. Date of Birth *(mm/dd/yyyy)*   **3. Sex** M F   **4. Place of Birth** *(City & State if in the U.S., or City & Country as it is presently known.)*

5. Social Security Number   **6. Email** *(Info alerts offered at* ***travel.state.gov****)* @   **7. Primary Contact Phone Number**

8. Mailing Address: Line 1: Street/RFD#, P.O. Box, or URB.

Address Line 2: **Clearly label** Apartment, Company, Suite, Unit, Building, Floor, In Care Of or Attention if applicable. *(e.g., In Care Of - Jane Doe, Apt # 100)*

City   State   Zip Code   Country, if outside the United States

9. List all other names you have used. *(Examples: Birth Name, Maiden, Previous Marriage, Legal Name Change. Attach additional pages if needed)*

A.   B.

Attach a color photograph taken within the last six months

10. Passport Book and/or Passport Card Information
Your name as printed on your most recent U.S. passport book and/or passport card

Most recent passport book number   Issue date *(mm/dd/yyyy)*

Most recent passport card number   Issue date *(mm/dd/yyyy)*

11. Name Change Information *Complete if name is different than last U.S. passport book or passport card*

Changed by Marriage   Place of Name Change *(City/State)*   Date *(mm/dd/yyyy)*

Changed by Court Order

Please submit a certified copy. **(Photocopies are not accepted!)**

➤ CONTINUE TO PAGE 2 ➤

YOU MUST SIGN AND DATE THE APPLICATION IN THE DESIGNATED AREA BELOW

I declare under penalty of perjury all of the following: 1) I am a citizen or non-citizen national of the United States and have not, since acquiring U.S. citizenship or nationality, performed any of the acts listed under "Acts or Conditions" on page four of the instructions of this application (unless explanatory statement is attached); 2) the statements made on the application are true and correct; 3) I have not knowingly and willfully made false statements or included false documents in support of this application; 4) the photograph submitted with this application is a genuine, current photograph of me; and 5) I have read and understood the warning on page one of the instructions to the application form.

X _______________________________
Applicant's Legal Signature   Date

FOR ISSUING OFFICE ONLY   ☐ PPT BK C/R   ☐ PPT BK S/R   ☐ PPT CD C/R   ☐ PPT CD S/R

☐ Marriage Certificate   Date of Marriage/Place Issued:

☐ Court Order   Date Filed/Court:

From _______________________________

To: _______________________________

☐ Other:

☐ Attached:

For Issuing Office Only ➤ Bk Fee____ Cd Fee____ EF____ Postage____ Other____

* DS 82 C 08 2013 1 *

DS-82 01-2017

Page 1 of 2

Name of Applicant *(Last, First & Middle)*	Date of Birth *(mm/dd/yyyy)*

12. Height	13. Hair Color	14. Eye Color	15. Occupation	16. Employer or School *(if applicable)*

17. Additional Contact Phone Numbers

	Home	Cell			Home	Cell
	Work				Work	

18. Permanent Address: *If P.O. Box is listed under Mailing Address __or__ if residence is different from Mailing Address.*

Street/RFD # or URB (*No P.O. Box*)   Apartment/Unit

City   State   Zip Code

19. Emergency Contact - *Provide the information of a person not traveling with you to be contacted in the event of an emergency.*

Name   Address: Street/RFD # or P.O. Box   Apartment/Unit

City   State   Zip Code   Phone Number   Relationship

20. Travel Plans

Departure Date *(mm/dd/yyyy)*   Return Date *(mm/dd/yyyy)*   Countries to be visited

STOP! YOU HAVE COMPLETED YOUR APPLICATION
BE SURE TO SIGN AND DATE PAGE ONE

WHERE DO I MAIL THIS APPLICATION?

If applying in the United States or Canada:

FOR ROUTINE SERVICE (If you live in CA, FL, IL, MN, NY, or TX):
National Passport Processing Center
P.O. Box 640155
Irving, TX 75064-0155

FOR ROUTINE SERVICE (If you live in any other state or Canada):
National Passport Processing Center
P.O. Box 90155
Philadelphia, PA 19190-0155

FOR EXPEDITED SERVICE (Additional Fee, any state or Canada):
National Passport Processing Center
P.O. Box 90955
Philadelphia, PA 19190-0955

Because of the sensitivity of the enclosed documents, Passport Services recommends using trackable mailing service when submitting your application.

If applying outside the United States or Canada:

United States citizens residing outside the U.S. or Canada **CANNOT** submit this form to domestic addresses listed above. Such applicants should visit www.usembassy.gov to find the nearest U.S. Embassy or Consulate for procedures for applying outside the United States.

* DS 82 C 08 2013 2 *

Appendix: Passport Application Form DS 5504

CORRECTIONS, NAME CHANGE WITHIN 1 YEAR OF PASSPORT ISSUANCE, AND LIMITED PASSPORT HOLDERS

PLEASE DETACH AND RETAIN THIS INSTRUCTION SHEET FOR YOUR RECORDS

Mailing Date of Application:______________________________

CAN I USE THIS FORM?

Complete this checklist to determine your eligibility to use this form

I have changed my name less than one year since my most recent U.S. passport book and/or U.S. passport card was issu**ed** **AND** my U.S. passport book and/or U.S. passport card is less than one year old;

☐ Yes ☐ No

OR

My identifying information in my most recent U.S. passport book and/or U.S. passport card was printed incorrectly;

☐ Yes ☐ No

OR

My most recent U.S. passport book was limited to two years or less for a reason other than multiple losses or a seriously damaged/mutilated passport.

☐ Yes ☐ No

If you answered NO to ALL of the three statements above, STOP - You cannot use this form!

You must apply on application form DS-11 or DS-82 depending on your circumstances. Please refer to those forms, visit **travel.state.gov**, or contact the National Passport Information Center for further information.

U.S. PASSPORTS, EITHER IN BOOK OR CARD FORMAT, ARE ISSUED ONLY TO U.S. CITIZENS OR NON-CITIZEN NATIONALS. EACH PERSON MUST OBTAIN HIS OR HER OWN PASSPORT BOOK OR PASSPORT CARD. THE PASSPORT CARD IS A U.S. PASSPORT ISSUED IN CARD FORMAT. LIKE THE TRADITIONAL PASSPORT BOOK, IT REFLECTS THE BEARER'S ORIGIN, IDENTITY, AND NATIONALITY AND IS SUBJECT TO EXISTING PASSPORT LAWS AND REGULATIONS. UNLIKE THE PASSPORT BOOK, THE PASSPORT CARD IS VALID ONLY FOR ENTRY TO THE UNITED STATES AT LAND BORDER CROSSINGS AND SEA PORTS OF ENTRY WHEN TRAVELING FROM CANADA, MEXICO, THE CARIBBEAN, AND BERMUDA. THE U.S. PASSPORT CARD IS NOT VALID FOR INTERNATIONAL AIR TRAVEL.

INFORMATION, QUESTIONS, AND INQUIRIES

Please visit our website at **travel.state.gov**. In addition, you may contact the National Passport Information Center (NPIC) toll-free at 1-877-487-2778 (TDD: 1-888-874-7793) or by email at **NPIC@state.gov**. Customer Service Representatives are available Monday-Friday 8:00a.m.-10:00p.m. Eastern Time (excluding federal holidays.) Automated information is available 24 hours a day, 7 days a week.

FAILURE TO PROVIDE INFORMATION REQUESTED ON THIS FORM, INCLUDING YOUR SOCIAL SECURITY NUMBER, MAY RESULT IN SIGNIFICANT PROCESSING DELAYS AND/OR THE DENIAL OF YOUR APPLICATION.

NOTICE TO APPLICANTS RESIDING ABROAD

United States citizens residing outside the U.S. or Canada **CANNOT** submit this form to the domestic address listed on the Instruction Page 2. Such applicants should contact the nearest U.S. Embassy or Consulate for procedures to be followed when applying overseas.

WARNING: False statements made knowingly and willfully in passport applications, including affidavits or other documents submitted to support this application, are punishable by fine and/or imprisonment under U.S. law, including the provisions of 18 U.S.C. 1001, 18 U.S.C. 1542, and/or 18 U.S.C. 1621. Alteration or mutilation of a passport issued pursuant to this application is punishable by fine and/or imprisonment under the provisions of 18 U.S.C. 1543. The use of a passport in violation of the restrictions contained therein or of the passport regulations is punishable by fine and/or imprisonment under 18 U.S.C. 1544. All statements and documents are subject to verification.

See page 2 of the instructions for detailed information on the completion and submission of this form.

If you choose to provide your email address in Item #6 on this application, Passport Services may use that information to contact you in the event there is a problem with your application or if additional information is required.

WHAT DO I SEND WITH THIS APPLICATION FORM?

1. **Your most recent U.S. passport book and/or passport card.**
2. **A recent color photograph.**

● Submit a color photograph of you alone, sufficiently recent to be a good likeness of you (taken within the last six months), and 2x2 inches in size. The image size measured from the bottom of your chin to the top of your head (including hair) should not be less than 1 inch, and not more than 1 3/8 inches. The photograph must be in color, clear, with a full front view of your face. The photograph must be taken with a neutral facial expression (preferred) or a natural smile, and with both eyes open and be printed on photo quality paper with a plain light (white or off-white) background. The photograph must be taken in normal street attire, without a hat or head covering unless a signed statement is submitted by the applicant verifying that the hat or head covering is part of recognized, traditional religious attire that is customarily or required to be worn continuously when in public or a signed doctor's statement is submitted verifying the item is used daily for medical purposes. Headphones, "bluetooth", or similar devices must not be worn in the passport photograph. Glasses or other eyewear are not acceptable unless you provide a signed statement from a doctor explaining why you cannot remove them due to medical reasons (e.g., during the recovery period from eye surgery). Any photograph retouched so that your appearance is changed is unacceptable. A snapshot, most vending machine prints, hand-held self portraits, and magazine or full-length photographs are unacceptable. A digital photo must meet the previously stated qualifications, and will be accepted for use at the discretion of Passport Services. Visit our website at **travel.state.gov** for details and information.

USE CAUTION WHEN STAPLING YOUR PHOTO: Use 4 staples vertically in the corners as close to the outer edges as possible. Do not bend the photo.

3. **Evidence to submit with this form (all documentary evidence that is not damaged, altered, or forged will be returned to you):**

● If your name has changed **less than one year** after your U.S. passport was issued **AND** your U.S. passport is **less than one year old**, you may use this form. You must submit a certified name change document such as a certified copy of your marriage certificate or a certified copy of a court order showing a seal and officiate/judge signature. If you are unable to document your name change in this manner, you must apply on the DS-11 application form by making a personal appearance at (1) a passport agency; (2) U.S. Embassy or Consulate, if abroad; (3) any federal or state court of record or any probate court accepting passport applications; (4) a designated municipal or county official; or (5) a post office, which has been selected to accept passport applications.

● If there is a name change or an error in the descriptive data in your recently issued, unexpired passport, you must submit the appropriate evidence showing the correct information (e.g. certified birth certificate or certified marriage certificate as described above).

● If you are re-applying because your U.S. passport book was limited in validity due to a lack of citizenship evidence or identity, you must submit evidence of your U.S. citizenship (such as a government-issued birth certificate or a U.S. Certificate of Naturalization) and/or evidence of your identity (such as a driver's license or a state issued identification card). You must establish your citizenship and identity to the satisfaction of Passport Services. We may ask you to provide additional evidence to corroborate your claim to U.S. citizenship and/or your identity. **Passports limited in validity due to serious damage or multiple losses cannot be extended.** Please contact the National Passport Information Center or visit **travel.state.gov** for more information and instructions.

● If your passport was limited due to gender transition, please visit **http://travel.state.gov/content/passports/en/passports/information/gender.html** for information on what documentation you will need to submit with this application form.

HOW DO I APPLY USING THIS FORM?

1. Complete, sign, and date this form.
2. Send this form with your most recent U.S. passport book and/or passport card, any required additional evidence, and a recent color photograph.

MAIL FORM TO:

FOR ROUTINE SERVICE:
National Passport Processing Center
Post Office Box 90107
Philadelphia, PA 19190-0107

FOR EXPEDITED SERVICE (Requires a Fee):
National Passport Processing Center
Post Office Box 90907
Philadelphia, PA 19190-0907

Because of the sensitivity of the enclosed documents, Passport Services recommends using trackable mailing service when submitting your application.

IS THERE A FEE ASSOCIATED WITH THIS FORM AND HOW WILL MY NEW U.S. PASSPORT BOOK AND/OR PASSPORT CARD BE MAILED BACK TO ME?

There is no fee associated with the use of this form unless expedited service is requested (see below). Your re-issued passport book and/or passport card and any documentary evidence submitted to Passport Services will be returned to you by priority or first class mail, unless overnight delivery is requested. You may receive your newly issued document and your returned citizenship evidence in separate mailings. If you are applying for both a U.S. passport book and card, you may receive **three separate mailings**: one with your returned citizenship evidence; one with your newly issued U.S. passport book, and one with your newly printed U.S. passport card.

OVERNIGHT DELIVERY SERVICE is only available for passport book (and not passport card) mailings in the United States. Please include the appropriate fee with your application.

For faster processing, you may request expedited service. Please include the expedite fee with your application. Expedited service is only available for passports mailed in the United States and Canada.

All fees must be submitted in the form of a personal check or money order. **MAKE CHECKS PAYABLE TO "U.S. DEPARTMENT OF STATE." THE FULL NAME AND DATE OF BIRTH OF THE APPLICANT MUST BE TYPED OR PRINTED ON THE FRONT OF THE CHECK. DO NOT SEND CASH.** Passport Services cannot be responsible for cash sent through the mail. Visit **travel.state.gov** for updated information on fees, processing times, or to check the status of your passport application online.

NOTE REGARDING MAILING ADDRESSES: Passport Services does not send mail to a private addresses outside the United States or Canada. If you do not live at the address listed in the "mailing address," then you must put the name of the person residing in that address and mark it as "In Care Of." If your mailing address changes prior to receipt of your new U.S. passport, please call the National Passport Information Center at 1-877-487-2778 or visit **travel.state.gov**.

NOTICE TO CUSTOMERS APPLYING OUTSIDE A DEPARTMENT OF STATE FACILITY

If you send us a check, it will be converted into an electronic funds transfer (EFT). This means we will copy your check, and use the account information on it to electronically debit your account for the amount of the check. The debit from your account will usually occur within 24 hours, and will be shown on your regular account statement.

You will not receive your original check back. We will destroy your original check, but we will keep the copy of it. If the EFT cannot be processed for technical reasons, you authorize us to process the copy in place of your original check. If the EFT cannot be completed because of insufficient funds, we may try to make the transfer up to two times, and we will charge you a one-time fee of $25, which we will also collect by EFT.

FEE REMITTANCE

Passport service fees are established by law and regulation (see 22 U.S.C. 214, 22 C.F.R. 22.1, and 22 C.F.R. 51.50-56) and are collected at the time you apply for the passport service. If the Department fails to receive full payment of the applicable fees because, for example, your check is returned for any reason or you dispute a passport fee charge to your credit card, the U.S. Department of State will take action to collect the delinquent fees from you under 22 C.F.R. Part 34, and the Federal Claims Collection Standards (see 31 C.F.R. Parts 900-904). In accordance with the Debt Collection Improvement Act (Pub.L. 104-134), if the fees remain unpaid after 180 days and no repayment arrangements have been made, the U.S. Department of State will refer the debt to the U.S. Department of Treasury for collection. Debt collection procedures used by the U.S. Department of Treasury may include referral of the debt to private collection agencies, reporting of the debt to credit bureaus, garnishment of private wages and administrative offset of the debt by reducing or withholding eligible federal payments (e.g., tax refunds, social security payments, federal retirement, etc.) by the amount of your debt, including any interest penalties or other costs incurred. In addition, non-payment of passport fees may result in the invalidation of your passport. An invalidated passport cannot be used for travel.

NOTICE TO APPLICANTS FOR OFFICIAL, DIPLOMATIC, OR NO-FEE PASSPORTS

You may use this application if you meet all of the provisions listed on Instruction Page 2; however, you must CONSULT YOUR SPONSORING AGENCY FOR INSTRUCTIONS ON PROPER ROUTING PROCEDURES BEFORE FORWARDING THIS APPLICATION. Your completed passport will be released to your sponsoring agency for forwarding to you.

IMPORTANT NOTICE TO APPLICANTS WHO HAVE LOST OR HAD A PREVIOUS U.S. PASSPORT BOOK AND/OR PASSPORT CARD STOLEN

A United States citizen may not normally bear more than one valid or potentially valid U.S. passport book or more than one valid or potentially valid U.S. passport card at a time. Therefore, when a valid or potentially valid U.S. passport book or U.S. passport card cannot be presented with a new application, it is necessary to submit a Form DS-64, Statement Regarding a Lost or Stolen U.S. Passport. Your statement must detail why the previous U.S. passport book or U.S. passport card cannot be presented.

The information you provide regarding your lost or stolen U.S. passport book or passport card will be placed into our Consular Lost or Stolen Passport System. This system is designed to prevent the misuse of your lost or stolen U.S. passport book or passport card. Anyone using the passport book or passport card reported as lost or stolen may be detained upon entry into the United States. Should you locate the U.S. passport book or passport card reported lost or stolen at a later time, report it as found, and submit it for cancellation. It has been invalidated. You may not use that passport book or passport card for travel.

PROTECT YOURSELF AGAINST IDENTITY THEFT!
REPORT YOUR LOST OR STOLEN PASSPORT BOOK OR PASSPORT CARD!

For more information or to report your lost or stolen U.S. passport book or passport card by phone, call NPIC or visit our website at **travel.state.gov**.

SPECIAL NOTICE TO U.S. PASSPORT CARD APPLICANTS ONLY

The maximum number of letters provided for your given name (first and middle) on the U.S. Passport Card is 24 characters. The 24 characters may be shortened due to printing restrictions. If both your given names are more than 24 characters, you must shorten the given name you list on item 1 of this form.

FEDERAL TAX LAW

Section 6039E of the Internal Revenue Code (26 U.S.C. 6039E) and 22 U.S.C 2714a(f) require you to provide your Social Security number (SSN), if you have one, when you apply for or renew a U.S. passport. If you have never been issued a SSN, you must enter zeros in box #5 of this form. If you are residing abroad, you must also provide the name of the foreign country in which you are residing. The U.S. Department of State must provide your SSN and foreign residence information to the U.S. Department of the Treasury. If you fail to provide the information, your application may be denied and you are subject to a $500 penalty enforced by the IRS. All questions on this matter should be referred to the nearest IRS office.

USE OF SOCIAL SECURITY NUMBER

Your Social Security number will be provided to U.S. Department of Treasury, used in connection with debt collection and checked against lists of persons ineligible or potentially ineligible to receive a U.S. passport, among other authorized uses.

ACTS OR CONDITIONS

If any of the below-mentioned acts or conditions have been performed by or apply to the applicant, the portion which applies should be lined out, and a supplementary explanatory statement under oath (or affirmation) by the applicant should be attached and made a part of this application.

I have not, since acquiring United States citizenship/nationality, been naturalized as a citizen of a foreign state; taken an oath or made an affirmation or other formal declaration of allegiance to a foreign state; entered or served in the armed forces of a foreign state; accepted or performed the duties of any office, post, or employment under the government of a foreign state or political subdivision thereof; made a formal renunciation of nationality either in the United States, or before a diplomatic or consular officer of the United States in a foreign state; or been convicted by a court or court martial of competent jurisdiction of committing any act of treason against, or attempting by force to overthrow, or bearing arms against, the United States, or conspiring to overthrow, put down, or to destroy by force, the government of the United States.

Furthermore, I have not been convicted of a federal or state drug offense or convicted for "sex tourism" crimes statute, and I am not the subject of an outstanding federal, state, or local warrant of arrest for a felony; a criminal court order forbidding my departure from the United States; a subpoena received from the United States in a matter involving federal prosecution for, or grand jury investigation of, a felony.

PRIVACY ACT STATEMENT

AUTHORITIES: Collection of this information is authorized by 22 U.S.C. 211a et seq.; 8 U.S.C. 1104; 26 U.S.C. 6039E, 22 U.S.C. 2714a(f), Section 236 of the Admiral James W. Nance and Meg Donovan Foreign Relations Authorization Act, Fiscal Years 2000 and 2001; Executive Order 11295 (August 5, 1966); and 22 C.F.R. parts 50 and 51.

PURPOSE: We are requesting this information in order to determine your eligibility to be issued a U.S. passport. Your Social Security number is used to verify your identity.

ROUTINE USES: This information may be disclosed to another domestic government agency, a private contractor, a foreign government agency, or to a private person or private employer in accordance with certain approved routine uses. These routine uses include, but are not limited to, law enforcement activities, employment verification, fraud prevention, border security, counterterrorism, litigation activities, and activities that meet the Secretary of State's responsibility to protect U.S. citizens and non-citizen nationals abroad. More information on the Routine Uses for the system can be found in System of Records Notices State-05, Overseas Citizen Services Records and State-26, Passport Records.

DISCLOSURE: Providing information on this form is voluntary. Be advised, however, that failure to provide the information requested on this form may cause delays in processing your U.S. passport application and/or could result in the refusal or denial of your application.

Failure to provide your Social Security number may result in the denial of your application (consistent with 22 U.S.C. 2714a(f)) and may subject you to a penalty enforced by the Internal Revenue Service, as described in the Federal Tax Law section of the instructions to this form. Your Social Security number will be provided to the Department of the Treasury and may be used in connection with debt collection, among other purposes authorized and generally described in this section.

ELECTRONIC PASSPORT STATEMENT

The U.S. Department of State now issues an "Electronic Passport" book, which contains an embedded electronic chip. The electronic passport book continues to be proof of the bearer's United States citizenship/nationality and identity, and looks and functions in the same way as a passport without a chip. The addition of an electronic chip in the back cover enables the passport book to carry a duplicate electronic copy of all information from the data page. The electronic passport book is usable at all ports-of-entry, including those that do not yet have electronic chip readers.

Use of the electronic format provides the traveler the additional security protections inherent in chip technology. Moreover, when used at ports-of-entry equipped with electronic chip readers, the electronic passport book provides for faster clearance through some of the port-of-entry processes.

The electronic passport book does not require special handling or treatment, but like previous versions should be protected from extreme heat, bending, and from immersion in water. The electronic chip must be read using specially formatted readers, which protects the data on the chip from unauthorized reading.

The cover of the electronic passport book is printed with a special symbol representing the embedded chip. The symbol  will appear in port-of-entry areas where the electronic passport book can be read.

PAPERWORK REDUCTION ACT STATEMENT

Public reporting burden for this collection of information is estimated to average 40 minutes per response, including the time required for searching existing data sources, gathering the necessary data, providing the information and/or documents required, and reviewing the final collection. You do not have to supply this information unless this collection displays a currently valid OMB control number. If you have comments on the accuracy of this burden estimate and/or recommendations for reducing it, please send them to: Passport Forms Officer, U.S. Department of State, CA/PPT/S/L, 44132 Mercure Cir, P.O. Box 1227, Sterling, Virginia 20166-1227.

APPLICATION FOR A U.S. PASSPORT

NAME CHANGE, DATA CORRECTION, AND LIMITED PASSPORT BOOK REPLACEMENT

Please Print Legibly Using Black Ink Only

OMB CONTROL NO.: 1405-0160
EXPIRATION DATE: 4-30-2021
ESTIMATED BURDEN: 40 MIN

Attention: Read WARNING on page 1 of instructions
Please select the document(s) for which you are applying:

☐ U.S. Passport Book ☐ U.S. Passport Card ☐ Both

The U.S. passport card is **not** valid for international air travel. For more information see page 1 of instructions.

☐ Regular Book (Standard) ☐ Large Book (Non-Standard)

Note: The large book option is for those who frequently travel abroad during the passport validity period and is recommended for applicants who have previously required the addition of visa pages.

☐ D ☐ O ☐ DP DOTS Code ____________
End. # ____________ Exp. ____________

1. Name Last

First

Middle

2. Date of Birth *(mm/dd/yyyy)*

3. Sex M F

4. Place of Birth *(City & State if in the U.S., or City & Country as it is presently known.)*

5. Social Security Number

6. Email *(Info alerts offered at **travel.state.gov**)* @

7. Primary Contact Phone Number

8. Mailing Address: Line 1: Street/RFD#, P.O. Box, or URB.

Address Line 2: **Clearly label** Apartment, Company, Suite, Unit, Building, Floor, In Care Of or Attention if applicable. *(e.g., In Care Of - Jane Doe, Apt # 100)*

City

State

Zip Code

Country, if outside the United States

9. List all other names you have used. *(Examples: Birth Name, Maiden, Previous Marriage, Legal Name Change. Attach additional pages if needed.)*

A.

B.

10. U.S. Passport Book and/or Passport Card Information

Your name as printed on your most recent U.S. passport book and/or passport card

Most recent U.S. passport book number

Book Issue Date *(mm/dd/yyyy)*

Most recent U.S. passport card number

Card Issue Date *(mm/dd/yyyy)*

━━ CONTINUE TO PAGE 2 ━━▶

YOU MUST SIGN AND DATE THE APPLICATION IN THE DESIGNATED AREA BELOW

I declare under penalty of perjury all of the following: 1) I am a citizen or non-citizen national of the United States and have not, since acquiring U.S. citizenship or nationality, performed any of the acts listed under "Acts or Conditions" on page four of the instructions of this application (unless explanatory statement is attached); 2) the statements made on the application are true and correct; 3) I have not knowingly and willfully made false statements or included false documents in support of this application; 4) the photograph submitted with this application is a genuine, current photograph of me; and 5) I have read and understood the warning on page one of the instructions to the application form.

X ____
Applicant's Legal Signature - age 16 and older

X ____
Mother/Father/Parent/Legal Guardian's Signature *(if identifying minor)*

____
Date

FOR ISSUING OFFICE ONLY

☐ Name Change ☐ Replacement ☐ Correction: LName FName MName DOB Sex POB Other

From: ____

To: ____

BC Nat/Citz Cert Report of Birth Prev PPT MC Adoption C/O NC C/O PIERS Other

Filed/Issued/Place: ________________ Doc #: ________________

☐ Other: ________________

☐ Attached: ________________

EF ________ Postage ________ Other ________

* DS 5504 C 11 2013 1 *

Name of Applicant *(Last, First & Middle)*

Date of Birth *(mm/dd/yyyy)*

11. Height

12. Hair Color

13. Eye Color

14. Occupation *(if age 16 or older)*

15. Employer or School *(if applicable)*

16. Additional Contact Phone Numbers

☐ Home ☐ Cell
☐ Work ___________

☐ Home ☐ Cell
☐ Work ___________

17. Permanent Address: *If P.O. Box is listed under Mailing Address* **or** *if residence is different from Mailing Address.*

Street/RFD # or URB (**No P.O. Box**)

Apartment/Unit

City

State

Zip Code

18. Emergency Contact - *Provide the information of a person not traveling with you to be contacted in the event of an emergency.*

Name

Address: Street/RFD # or P.O. Box

Apartment/Unit

City

State

Zip Code

Phone Number

Relationship

19. Travel Plans

Departure Date *(mm/dd/yyyy)*   Return Date *(mm/dd/yyyy)*   Countries to be visited

Please complete the following questions regarding your current passport book and/or passport card

Has your name changed by marriage or court order less than one year after your U.S. passport book or passport card was issued?

☐ Yes   ☐ No

If yes, **and your submitted passport book and/or passport card is less than one year old**, please complete this section with your current information.

Current Name Last

First

Middle

Note: You must **submit evidence documenting your name change** (such as a certified marriage certificate or court order) and your current U.S. passport book and/or passport card, along with this completed form to the address listed on page 2 of the instructions.

If you can not or did not meet the above criteria, please complete Form DS-82, U.S. Passport Renewal Application for Eligible Individuals or Form DS-11, Application for a U.S. Passport.

Was your identifying information printed incorrectly in your U.S. passport book or passport card?

☐ Yes   ☐ No

If yes, please complete the information as it should appear, and **check only the box(s) next to the field(s) to be corrected.**

☐ **Name** Last

☐ First

☐ Middle

☐ **Date of Birth** *(mm/dd/yyyy)*

☐ **Sex**
☐ M
☐ F

☐ **Place of Birth** *(State or Country)*

Please submit evidence documenting your correct identifying information (such as a certified marriage certificate or birth certificate) and your current U.S. passport book and/or passport card, along with this completed form to the address listed on page 2 of the instructions.

Was your most recent U.S. passport limited for two years or less?

☐ Yes   ☐ No

If yes, please submit evidence of your U.S. citizenship (such as a U.S. birth certificate or naturalization certificate) and/or evidence of your identity (such as a driver's license or a state-issued ID card). Visit **http://travel.state.gov/content/passports/en/passports/information/gender.html** for information regarding gender transition documentation.

Note: To complete a limited U.S. passport book replacement, **your submitted U.S. passport book must not be expired.** Passport books limited in validity because of multiple losses, damages, or mutilations **cannot be extended.**

Please be sure to enclose your U.S. passport book along with this application to the address listed on page 2 of the instructions.

Appendix: Voter Registration Application

Voter Registration Application

Before completing this form, review the General, Application, and State specific instructions.

<table>
<tr><td colspan="2">
Are you a citizen of the United States of America?   ☐ Yes   ☐ No
Will you be 18 years old on or before election day?   ☐ Yes   ☐ No
If you checked "No" in response to either of these questions, do not complete form.
(Please see state-specific instructions for rules regarding eligibility to register prior to age 18.)
</td><td>This space for office use only.</td></tr>
</table>

#					
1	☐ Mr. ☐ Miss ☐ Mrs. ☐ Ms. Last Name	First Name	Middle Name(s)	☐ Jr ☐ Sr ☐ II ☐ III ☐ IV	
2	Home Address	Apt. or Lot #	City/Town	State	Zip Code
3	Address Where You Get Your Mail If Different From Above		City/Town	State	Zip Code

4 Date of Birth _____ Month Day Year	**5** Telephone Number (optional)	**6**	ID Number - (See item 6 in the instructions for your state)
7 Choice of Party (see item 7 in the instructions for your State)	**8** Race or Ethnic Group (see item 8 in the instructions for your State)		___________________

9

I have reviewed my state's instructions and I swear/affirm that:
- I am a United States citizen
- I meet the eligibility requirements of my state and subscribe to any oath required.
- The information I have provided is true to the best of my knowledge under penalty of perjury. If I have provided false information, I may be fined, imprisoned, or (if not a U.S. citizen) deported from or refused entry to the United States.

Please sign full name (or put mark) ▲

Date: _____ / _____ / _____
   Month   Day   Year

If you are registering to vote for the first time: please refer to the application instructions for information on submitting copies of valid identification documents with this form.

Please fill out the sections below if they apply to you.

If this application is for a **change of name**, what was your name before you changed it?

A	☐ Mr. ☐ Miss ☐ Mrs. ☐ Ms. Last Name	First Name	Middle Name(s)	☐ Jr ☐ Sr ☐ II ☐ III ☐ IV

If you were **registered before but this is the first time you are registering from the address in Box 2**, what was your address where you were registered before?

	Street (or route and box number)	Apt. or Lot #	City/Town/County	State	Zip Code
B					

If you live in a rural area but do not have a street number, or if you have no address, please show on the map where you live.

C
- Write in the names of the crossroads (or streets) nearest to where you live.
- Draw an X to show where you live.
- Use a dot to show any schools, churches, stores, or other landmarks near where you live, and write the name of the landmark.

NORTH ↑

Example

Route #2

● Grocery Store

Woodchuck Road

Public School ●

X

If the applicant is unable to sign, who helped the applicant fill out this application? Give name, address and phone number (phone number optional).

D	

Mail this application to the address provided for your State.